HISPANIC PERSONALITIES

Celebrities of the Spanish-speaking World

By GARY WOHL
and CARMEN CADILLA RUIBAL

REGENTS PUBLISHING COMPANY, INC.

Published by
Regents Publishing Company, Inc.
2 Park Avenue
New York, N.Y. 10016

Printed in the United States of America

ISBN 0-88345-302-9   985

TABLE OF CONTENTS

PREFACE

This book is intended for students of English as a second language—especially those of Hispanic descent—at both the intermediate and advanced levels. It is equally useful for native speakers of English in remedial reading English classes.

It has been our purpose, however, to go beyond the above stated objectives in order to reach the general reader as well. With this end in mind, we offer a collection of biographical sketches of some of the distinguished personalities of the Spanish-speaking world. Political activists, writers, sportsmen, scientists, etc., are represented here. Much to our regret, many names and entire fields of human activity have been excluded, since the book is just a reader with the specific aim of teaching a language, and not a comprehensive cultural work. It is our hope, however, that these sketches will stimulate the interest of the reader (regardless of ethnic descent) in Hispanic culture, and will encourage him or her to explore the subject further.

The brevity of the sketches serves a pedagogical aim, namely, that each of them can be dealt with in the time allotted for a class period. Study aids such as vocabulary drills, sequencing, comprehension, and activity questions supplement the sketches.

In short, the purpose of this book is twofold: to teach the English language and to introduce the reader to one of the great cultures of the world. We hope we have fulfilled these aims.

ACKNOWLEDGMENTS

This book would not have been possible without the work of Yolanda Fuchs, Lana Kaye, and Jerry Labinger, who generously contributed their time and energy. Special thanks to Rosalie Hollingsworth for her translations. My deepest appreciation to my editor, Roberta West, for her understanding, sensitivity, and expertise.

For Irving, Renée, Harriet, with love

1

CIRO ALEGRÍA

Interpreter of the Indian Soul

The South American Indian, his problems as a human being, and the relentless exploitation he has suffered under the white man, are the themes of Alegría's novels. Wrapped in the poetic context of the Andean panorama, he gave the world an interpretation of the Indian as a man, rather than as an exotic, picturesque creature devoid of sensitivity and human needs.

Ciro Alegría was born in 1909 at his parents' hacienda in a province of Peru. Since early childhood he was greatly influenced by his maternal grandmother, a mestiza of Irish and Indian blood who read him stories, legends, and myths of the Andes and its people. Later, as a teenager, helping his father manage the family property, he shared a rural life with the Indians he already loved and understood. He often took with him on his long horseback journeys a little Indian called Gaspar who would follow him on his mule, playing an Inca flute, the *antara*.

At school, Ciro was further influenced by a teacher who turned out to be the great Peruvian poet, César Vallejo, himself a champion of the South American Indian. As is often the case with Latin American intellectuals, Alegría developed an early interest in politics as a means to achieve justice and liberation for the oppressed. For those activities he suffered jail since the age of twenty-one. Several times he was banished into exile. While living in Chile in exile, he wrote his first major novel, *La serpiente de oro*, which won a literary prize in Argentina. The book was translated into several languages including German, but it didn't get published then in Germany. The Hitler regime found it contrary to its racist principles, since the novel was about Indians and mestizos.

Banished again to Chile for his political writings, Alegría wrote his second novel while convalescing from a serious illness. The book, entitled *Los perros hambrientos*, won Ciro another literary prize. It describes the life of the Andean shepherds, their struggles for survival against the mountain storms, and the hazards of their work and existence. In it he has a character called Pancho, a child shepherd who plays a little flute—much like Gaspar had done for Ciro years before.

In 1941 Alegría won a literary prize in the United States with his best-known novel, *El mundo es ancho y ajeno*. He remained in New York for several years, teaching at Columbia University and writing for American publications. The University of Puerto Rico invited him in 1947 to teach a course on Latin American literature, and that started Alegría's love affair with the island.

During his last years, Alegría wandered through Latin America, living in poverty. He was not a businessman; he would sign contracts without reading them, glad enough to find a publisher interested in printing his books. He continued his involvement in Peruvian social struggles on behalf of the downtrodden Indian who had inspired almost every word he wrote. Finally, after a long illness, he died in his native land, in 1967.

In *Los perros hambrientos* there is a twelve-year-old Indian girl called La Antuca who stops along the Andean cordillera and says to herself:

> The Sun is my father
> The Earth is my mother,
> My sisters are the Stars.
>
> Ah, love, little love,
> Come to me if you do exist.
> I wander in the world alone,
> No one knows about me.

2

ALICIA ALONSO

Cuban Ballerina and Choreographer

Latin America has given the world some of the best dancers performing at present—including one of the greatest ballerinas of all time: Alicia Alonso.

Alicia Martínez began studying ballet in her native Havana. At the age of fifteen she fell in love with a fellow-pupil, Fernando Alonso, and ran off with him to the United States, both bent on pursuing a ballet career. They got married in New York, where their daughter, Laura, their only child, was born. While Alicia's mother took care of the baby in their uptown Manhattan apartment, the young parents made a living dancing in New York musicals, while training for ballet. Eventually they joined a ballet company. From the start it was obvious that the budding Cuban ballerina was star material; she had beauty, line, technique, elevation, and a natural ability to *act* as well as dance a role. (In time she was to thrill audiences with her dramatic *Giselle* and equally delight the young with her mischievous *Coppelia.*)

At the height of her early success Alicia had to undergo an eye operation that required a year of convalescence in bed, in a darkened room. (Imagine what would happen to an athlete if he had to spend a year without training or even walking!) Alicia kept the record player going through her confinement, reviewing in her mind the choreographies she yearned to dance again. As soon as her doctors allowed it she went back to her classes and rehearsals, eager to make up for the year she had lost. Soon she joined her company again, the American Ballet Theatre.

One day, when *Giselle* had been scheduled for the evening, the star fell ill and Alicia had to take over the role. She made front-page headlines the next morning: an extraordinary artist had been discovered. Stardom, European tours, and one of the highest salaries in ballet followed in a few short years. Alicia Alonso became the United States *assoluta,* as each country calls its greatest ballerina. Still, she managed to perform often in her beloved Cuba, although New York continued to be her first home and base of operations.

In 1960 the Alonsos decided to move back to Cuba and form a permanent company. They had to start by establishing a ballet school in each of the island's six provinces in order to develop a grass-roots source of dancers. The struggle was titanic, but by 1966 Cuban dancers were winning medals and prizes in international ballet competitions in Europe. The Cuban National Ballet, headed by its star and founder, performed all over the world, except in the United States. Until recently, Cuban Alicia Alonso was the world's only ballerina not allowed to perform for American audiences because of her communist affiliation.

All that was changed in the summer of 1975. In a magnificent gesture of international cooperation between the governments of the United States and Cuba, Alicia Alonso performed once again in the city that had made her a star, New York, in a gala performance with her mother company, the American Ballet Theatre, at Lincoln Center. She danced *Swan Lake* with her Cuban partner, young Jorge Esquivel, a winner at Varna's international competition, the world's top ballet festival. They received an eighteen-minute standing ovation, the longest in the memory of the critics, according to *The New York Times*. A ten-yard flag was unfurled from the first balcony, with the words: "Welcome, Alicia, *Bienvenida*." Alicia Alonso had New York at her feet, and so many flowers that her partner had to sweep her in his arms over the mound so she could be seen taking her bows. A Puerto Rican journalist, Rafael Rodríguez, called the event: "Alice in Wonderland."

Next day at a press conference, before taking her plane back to Havana, she said into the microphones and television cameras: "Art has no frontiers. Art belongs to the world, and the world is you and me."

3

MIGUEL ÁNGEL ASTURIAS

"I write to the tread of barefoot Indian feet."

Although he spent much of his life outside his native Guatemala, Miguel Ángel Asturias is considered to be his country's greatest twentieth-century writer. He lived many years in Paris, first as a student, later as a diplomat, and finally as a retired private citizen. Yet his self-imposed exile did not mean that he was indifferent to his country, for few modern writers have shown as much feeling for their homeland as Asturias did.

Asturias saw himself as a symbol of Indo-American man, a man, he believed, who got his power from the earth. He thought that the earth was the mother of all life and that all human mothers were linked to the earth in the natural order of things. He once said, "the mother is the great sorceress, the great healer, the greatest of all the stars."

Asturias admired the native Indian farmers of Guatemala. "These farmers may be poor and without power today," he said, "but they can be proud of their ancient past." The heritage he spoke of is the great Mayan civilization that ruled Central America for several centuries. Asturias was part Indian himself; he said that he wrote as a native and not as a Spaniard. He not only bore physical traces of his Mayan ancestry, but he was also quiet and calm, and he listened more than he spoke. This stoic bearing caused some people to compare him to an ancient Mayan chief.

His first book, published in 1930, was called *Leyendas de Guatemala.* It is a collection of stories that come partly from old legends, partly from everyday events in his childhood, and partly from the tales his mother made up for him when he was a boy. Asturias said about this book, "I was expressing my devotion to my country, to my little native land, to my little corner of volcanoes, lakes, mountains, clouds, birds, and flowers."

Asturias' works are not confined to myths and ancient Indian tales. His best-known novel, *El señor presidente,* is based on the terror he experienced during a bloody and repressive dictatorship in Guatemala when he was a child. The book was published in 1946, right after the fall of the Nazi dictatorship in Europe.

In this novel, Asturias develops the theme that the fight for political freedom is a struggle of good against evil, symbolized by light against darkness. Famous for its symbolism and the sonorous mimicry of the tolling church bells which follows, the marvelous opening sentence unforgettably sets the theme: *"Alumbra, lumbre de alumbre, Luzbel de piedralumbre."*

In another beautifully written passage, Asturias describes the feelings of a woman being taken by carriage to the palace of the president, who had had her husband arrested and is about to have him shot. "The vehicle did not move, she felt that it was not moving, that the wheels turned on sleeping axles without going forward, always on the same spot, and she had to save her husband. Yes, yes, yes, yes, yes,—her hair fell loose—save him."

She failed to save him, and the president continued to rule and slaughter those who opposed him, but even when the enemy of freedom wins a temporary victory, Asturias leaves the reader with the impression that freedom and justice will eventually prevail.

Asturias believed passionately in democracy, and when Guatemala's democratic government was overthrown by a military coup in 1954, he left for other parts of Latin America. His next work after *El señor presidente* was a trilogy about the workers on the banana plantations of Guatemala. *Viento fuerte, El papa verde*, and *Los ojos de los enterrados* tell the story of how exploited campesinos fought against the power of the huge American-controlled plantations that ruthlessly ruled their lives.

When asked which of his books he liked best, Asturias named another book about life in Guatemala, saying, "One loves one's books as one loves one's children, but the one I like best is *Hombres de maíz*, although I recognize that *El señor presidente* is a book of literary importance. *Hombres de maíz* is a more obscure book. . . . It can be read as a novel, but it is profound, too."

In 1967 Asturias won the Nobel Prize for Literature, the most prestigious honor accorded any writer in the world. When asked what the award meant to him, he replied with characteristic modesty, "I never thought that I should be awarded the prize, although my name was mentioned year after year. I thought it must have been given to Rómulo Gallegos, who certainly deserved it. I was one of those who signed a request to the academy on his behalf."

After democratic government was restored to Guatemala, Asturias served in various diplomatic posts, eventually becoming Ambassador to France, where he retired. He died in Madrid, June 9, 1974.

4

HERMAN BADILLO

Up from Poverty

Herman Badillo is a living example of how it is possible for a poor Puerto Rican immigrant in New York City to become successful.

The early years of this proud, hardworking man were filled with misfortune. He was born in Caguas, Puerto Rico, in 1929. His father died only one year later, and his mother died when he was five. The young orphan was then raised by his aunt, Aurelia.

They were poor, but Herman developed a strong will to succeed. "I'm proud and I've always been proud," he recently said. "After my parents died, I was starving, but I wouldn't go to the square to beg with the other children." Instead while attending the Luis Muñoz Rivera primary school, Herman earned pennies by cleaning floors.

When he was eleven, his aunt brought him to New York City. They rented an apartment in *El Barrio*, (Spanish Harlem) and Herman entered the public school on East 103rd Street. In the years ahead, he struggled to get a good education. He supported himself while attending Harlem High School and City College by working nights as a short order cook, a dishwasher, and a pinboy in a bowling alley.

He was admitted to the Bar in 1954 after graduating *cum laude* (with honors) from Brooklyn Law School. He quickly became a certified public accountant. Later he moved to the South Bronx, which was rapidly becoming a Puerto Rican community, and entered politics.

His first real break came when Mayor Wagner chose him as deputy real estate commissioner. He soon became commissioner of relocation and, in 1965, won election as borough president in the Bronx. He was, by this time, the most promising politician of Puerto Rican birth in the United States.

When Badillo was elected to the Ninety-second Congress in 1971, he became the first Puerto Rican ever to hold a voting membership in that body, and he vowed to represent the people of Puerto Rico as well as those of his New York district. (The island of Puerto Rico sends its resident commissioner to the House of Representatives, but he does not vote.) When the freshman Congressman was appointed to the Agriculture Committee, a furor broke out; a *New York Times* editorial (February 1, 1971) called the appointment "an insulting waste of Badillo's talents and his experience."

When Badillo challenged the assignment in the House's Democratic caucus, he succeeded in being transferred to the Education and Labor Committee, which also handles most antipoverty legislation. In his first major speech on the House floor, Badillo asked the Federal Government to lend $20 billion to America's cities until a federal revenue-sharing program could be enacted.

He set his sights on becoming the first Hispanic mayor of New York City, and in 1973 he entered the Democratic primary against three other candidates. Congressman Badillo had always been a liberal, backing the rights of the poor, fighting against discrimination, and speaking against the war in Vietnam. In his mayoral campaign, however, he stressed the need to unite all

New Yorkers, both middle class and poor, in an effort to solve the city's problems.

The city's survival, Badillo said, depends upon leadership "that can talk and work with every group and community, that can build coalitions so people can think and work in terms of those hopes and dreams they hold in common." Badillo did lose the election, but he will probably try again.

Among his many programs, he supports methadone maintenance for drug addicts, and he helped found the city's only bilingual drug program, *SERA*.

Herman Badillo has with reason called himself a "one-man integration ticket." He himself is Baptist. His wife is Jewish.

Badillo, who is 6'1" tall, has often expressed resentment at being called a "tall Puerto Rican," maintaining that poor diet and extreme poverty prevent most of his people from growing taller. He has told interviewers that he grew six inches the first summer he was in the United States, having had not "more than three gallons of milk or four dozen eggs" during the previous six years.

Badillo is considered a reserved man who is difficult to know. During the mayoral campaign, an aide told Fred Ferretti of *New York* magazine, "Badillo thinks he doesn't need anybody. It's not arrogance. It's rather . . . a belief in his destiny."

5

RAMÓN EMETERIO BETANCES

Doctor, Scholar, Humanitarian, Rebel

Ramón Emeterio Betances was born on April 8, 1827, in a large and comfortable house near the town of Cabo Rojo, Puerto Rico. Almost from the day he began to walk, the boy was drawn to his father's library. Instead of playing with toys or puzzles, as his sisters and brothers did, he learned how to read. His mother died when he was eleven years old, and he sought comfort in his books.

As Betances reached adolescence, he openly began to advocate both the end of slavery and Puerto Rican independence. Afraid that his son would become involved in the separatist movement and end up in prison, his father sent him to study in France.

Betances went to school in Toulouse, where he wrote his first poems and essays. In 1848 he received his baccalaureate degree and returned to Puerto Rico for a vacation. When he arrived, he visited his older sister, Clara, and found that his niece, María del Carmen Henri, had become a beautiful young woman. He fell madly in love with her, and she with him. In his life, he would have two great loves, this woman and his country.

The desire to serve his country in the best possible way moved Betances to enroll at the Sorbonne, the famous university in Paris, where he specialized in the study of tropical diseases. In his free time he became friendly with the artists of the Montmartre district. He wrote theatrical pieces, poems, novels, and articles, all in perfect French, which earned him a considerable literary and scientific reputation.

After finishing his studies, Betances returned to Puerto Rico and settled in the city of Mayagüez. His sweetheart was near him, he was living in his homeland, and with the aid of a friend, Segundo Ruiz Belvis, he was able to buy the freedom of slave children. The young doctor's happiness was nearly complete.

In 1856 one of the most disastrous events in the history of the island occurred. A cholera epidemic erupted and spread rapidly. For weeks, Betances fought desperately to save lives, even at the risk of losing his own. He scarcely slept, and he often went for days without a meal. The unsanitary conditions of the over-crowded slave huts were sources of infection, so Betances ordered them burned. He separated the healthy from the sick, and by using the proper medication and hygiene methods, he managed to save many lives.

The epidemic cost over 30,000 lives. When it was over, Betances dedicated himself completely to scientific and humanitarian work. He established hospitals and schools throughout Puerto Rico and helped the needy in every possible way. For his dedication and selflessness, he was named *El padre de los pobres*. The Spanish government wanted to honor him for his work, but he refused. He would not accept rewards from those who oppressed his country.

In addition to being a doctor and a writer, Betances was a man of action who could not remain indifferent to political unrest and social injustices. In 1858, after working openly for the freedom of slaves and the right of his country to a better government, he was ordered by the governor to leave the island. Before leaving, he became engaged to his beloved Carmelita. They made plans to be married in Paris the following May.

The bride-to-be arrived from Puerto Rico in March 1859. Betances was already working and his scientific reputation was opening doors for him. But he could not enjoy his blessings while his country continued to suffer under the colonial yoke. An even greater anguish awaited him, however, one from which he would never recover completely. On April 24, his fiancée died from typhoid fever in Paris. Betances sank into a profound depression. In September he brought his wife's body to the Caribbean to be buried in their homeland.

Gradually, with the help of his family and friends, Betances overcame his grief. He resumed medical practice in Mayagüez and continued his humanitarian activities.

In 1867 the Puerto Rican delegates to the Spanish Parliament moved for the abolition of slavery on the island. Betances and his old friend, Segundo Ruiz Belvis, organized movements not only to abolish slavery, but also to win the independence of Puerto Rico by force. During this period, a riot broke out in the military barracks in San Juan. Although they had nothing to do with this uprising, Betances, Ruiz Belvis, and other patriots were sentenced to exile. However, Betances and Belvis escaped in a boat and landed in Santo Domingo. From there they went to New York City, where they continued their labors, trying to buy weapons and recruit men for the revolution. Eventually, Ruiz Belvis went to Chile, but Betances returned to Santo Domingo, where he married his former housekeeper, Simplicia Jiménez. He obtained enough money there to buy munitions and a schooner, *El Telégrafo*, which was to be sent to Puerto Rico at the hour of need.

When the Dominican government learned of the plans, Betances was forced to seek asylum in the United States Consulate,

together with several members of his family and a number of
friends, but they were all taken prisoner. A few days later a
Dominican government official became gravely ill, and he asked
Dr. Betances to attend him. Betances refused to do so unless he
and his entire party were freed. The request was granted and he
cured the official, but the Dominican government continued to
persecute him. Betances then declared his intention to become an
American citizen and was given protection by the American Consulate. Eventually, however, Betances changed his mind and took
up Dominican citizenship instead.

After four years of exile from Puerto Rico, Betances returned to Paris. Friends from Montmartre received him joyously. He spent part of his time there engaged in scientific studies, and he continued his work in medicine, founding schools and hospitals, and writing articles. Cuban and Dominican revolutionists named him their diplomatic representative in Paris.

In 1893 Betances' health began to fail. He was poor, ill, and depressed, but he devoted his last years to the liberation of Cuba. He hoped that with the help of the other Antilles, Puerto Rico too would become free.

When the United States declared war on Spain, the Puerto Rican patriot was almost an invalid. He lived through the anguishing results of the Treaty of Paris, by which Spain ceded the government of Puerto Rico to the United States. His homeland still was not free.

On September 16, 1898, Ramón Emeterio Betances died in France. He will always be remembered, in France and the Antilles, as a romantic revolutionary, an international humanitarian, and an outstanding Puerto Rican.

6

SIMÓN BOLÍVAR

Venezuelan Liberator of South America

His statue stands in hundreds of public squares, his portrait hangs on the walls of public buildings, and coins bear his name. Five Republics call him the father of their independence, and one country, Bolivia, was named after him. Yet he himself did not live to see South America liberated and united. He died a broken and embittered man.

Simón Bolívar was born in Caracas, Venezuela, July 24, 1783. Though born into a wealthy, aristocratic family, his early life was full of disappointments. His father died when he was only three and his mother died six years later. When he was twenty-two, his young Spanish bride died of yellow fever. Perhaps these early misfortunes turned him inward, deepening his interest in political philosophy and the welfare of his people. Simón was an unruly, temperamental child who disliked taking orders and preferred to be his own master. His uncle, Don Carlos Palacios, managed his inheritance and engaged his tutors. One tutor did reach this impetuous adolescent. He was Simón Rodríguez, himself an eccentric personality and disciple of the liberal French educator Jean-Jacques Rousseau. Bolívar was inspired by Rousseau's innovative philosophy and love of freedom. That inspiration would turn his sights toward the French and the American revolutions and thus change the destiny of South America.

The name "Bolívar" is Basque, the family originating in the village of Bolívar in northern Spain, between San Sebastián and Bilbao.

Simón Bolívar was a pale-skinned, slender youth with quick, nervous movements and a strong temper. He was five feet six inches tall. His high forehead was deeply lined, even in his early youth. His eyes were coal-black and piercing. As a young man he wore long sideburns and a mustache. He was a great charmer and lover of women, with an old-fashioned chivalry quite appropriate for a nobleman. However, he did not remarry after his wife's death.

Bolívar's personality was a calm one, but he became suddenly violent at times. He often spent long hours lying on his hammock with a book of Jean-Jacques Rousseau. In fact, this born aristocrat usually slept in a hammock, on a cowhide on the floor, or out-of-doors wrapped in his cloak, seldom more than five or six hours a night. Besides reading, he loved horseback riding, dancing, and lots of exercise in the countryside. In spite of his gaunt look, Simón had boundless energy. He loved fine wines and champagne, but he did nothing in excess, except spend money on parties and gifts for his friends. In this alone he was lavish. Bolívar was scrupulously neat. In the tropics, he bathed three times a day. He hated drunkards, gamblers, and gossips, and considered friendship sacred.

Though he had a taste for pomp and elegant parties, he also loved the simple things in life: a plain Indian stew and a ride on the open plains, for instance. He also distrusted excessive flattery or formality and enjoyed a good joke. Once, upon arriving at a village after a long march, he was greeted by a young intellectual who took a sheaf of papers out of his pocket and began to read a seemingly interminable oration. The young man came to the part that read, "When Caesar crossed the Rubicon, . . ." and Bolívar interrupted, "My dear friend, when Caesar crossed the Rubicon he had had breakfast. I have not yet had mine. Let us first have breakfast."

Though of a rebellious temperament as a youth, Bolívar nevertheless became very well-educated, partly by reading the classics, such as Plutarch's *Lives*, and the literature of the French Revolution. He loved oratory and was a powerful speaker, able to influence people and draw them to his side through careful logic.

Bolívar's gift of expression was not limited to Spanish. He spoke and wrote French and Italian fluently and could also read English. Although his heart remained with his own Hispanic-American people, his outlook was international. He sought guidance and aid from both Europe and the United States in his plans for liberation.

Bolívar's courage and shrewdness did not wither under adversity. On the contrary, after his first attempt to liberate Venezuela failed, he merely devised an ingenious new strategy and was soon back on the battlefront. This born fighter was able to withstand all kinds of adverse conditions—cold, hunger, fatigue,—in order to defeat his enemies.

The American Revolution had inspired him with a very unusual idea—a "United States of Hispanic America", an idea that kept him and his men marching and fighting day and night against overwhelming obstacles.

Bolívar is the subject of many biographies, some favorable, some not. At least he is a very controversial figure. Vicente Lecuna, a Venezuelan author, considered him the greatest military leader in history, whereas Salvador de Madariaga pictured him as a scheming opportunist who forgot his ideals when they got in the way of personal gain. Venezuelan scholar J. L. Salcedo-Bastardo credits Bolívar with agrarian land reform because he gave conquered land to peasant soldiers who had supported him.

At the age of twenty-one, Bolívar began to think deeply about his own personal identity. He would soon identify with the newly crowned emperor Napoleon Bonaparte. He admired Napoleon's authoritarian ways, but later despised him for his lack of faith in revolutionary ideals. Then one day in Rome, after having read Voltaire and Montesquieu, Bolívar stood on a hilltop and vowed to liberate his country from colonial oppression. When Napoleon invaded Spain and deposed the king, Simón Bolívar knew that the time had come to break ties with the Iberian Peninsula and liberate South America. He moved swiftly, enlisting the aid of exiled patriot Francisco de Miranda, who had previously attempted a revolution. Miranda returned to Caracas to command the independence movement. The first campaign was unsuccessful. Miranda was captured and had to spend the rest of his life in Spanish dungeons. Bolívar fled to Colombia after the defeat and the terrible earthquake of 1812. However, he was determined to strike again with even more force and cunning. The next battle for Venezuelan freedom also failed when the Spanish successfully enlisted the *llaneros,* cowboys of the Orinoco Valley. These were undisciplined but fierce men, difficult to beat.

Having failed again, Bolívar fled to Jamaica, physically exhausted and discouraged, but not defeated. He had lost his money and possessions, but had a few friends there who supported him. He tried to obtain aid for his cause from Great Britain. It was from Jamaica that he wrote with optimism, "A people that love freedom will in the end be free. We are a microcosm of the human race. We are a world apart, confined within two oceans, young in the arts and sciences, but old as any human society. We are neither Indians nor Europeans, yet we are a part of each." Envisioning one large constitutional republic modeled on that of Great Britain, he looked forward to achieving "a United Hispanic America," free of foreign rule.

In 1817, with native troops back on his side along with several thousand British and Irish soldiers, he launched one of the most daring attacks in military history. Engaging the popular revolutionary leader of the Orinoco Valley, José Páez, he approached the royalist troops from the rear. It was on the plains of New Granada that the first and most decisive victory was won. But before this victory, Bolívar lost many of his men in marches through swamps and over the Andes where they died of disease, froze to death, or fell over precipices in the dark. The turning point in the history of northern South America came when that ragged, starving horde swooped down from those "impassable" Andes ridges upon unsuspecting royalist troops of New Granada, who were forced to surrender at the Battle of Boyacá on August 7, 1819. New Granada became *La República de Colombia* in December 1819. Francisco de Paula Santander became vice president, and this government was recognized by the United States.

Venezuela became a free country at last after the famous battle of Carabobo in 1821. By the end of the year Ecuador was also liberated, with the invaluable assistance of one of Bolívar's ablest officers, Antonio José de Sucre.

In Quito, Bolívar's heart was won by the beautiful and vivacious Manuela Sáenz, a provocative mixture of Amazon and courtesan. A passionate revolutionary, she accompanied him both on the battlefield and into the presidential palace.

In the meantime, José de San Martín had been trying to liberate southern Peru. It was rumored that there had been rivalry between him and Bolívar, who was a colorful, youthful egotist, whereas San Martín was stoic, taciturn, and modest. San Martín voluntarily went into exile, and in 1823 Bolívar, assisted by Sucre, moved his men, horses, mules, and ammunition into the high mountain country of Peru. After the first major battle of Junín, the Spanish viceroy surrendered.

By then, Bolívar was "Liberator" and president of both Colombia and Peru. In April of 1825, Upper Peru fell to Sucre. This region became Bolivia, named after the Liberator himself. The conqueror then drafted a new constitution, but *not* one patterned after its British counterpart, as he had hoped. Bolívar's fear of secession, counter-revolution, civil wars, and assassination plots led him to establish a lifetime presidency, a legislative body without real power, and greatly restricted suffrage.

Although he had reached the pinnacle of his career, his dream of a totally united South America had not been realized. However, a League of Hispanic-American States convened in Panama in 1826 and was internationally recognized.

With his characteristic grandiose thinking, Bolívar had his mind on the continent. But, the aims of other Latin American leaders and their peoples were basically regional.

Bolívar's fears of dissension and assassination were well-grounded. In 1828 a group of liberal conspirators entered his palace and attempted to murder him, but Manuela Sáenz saved his life. After he lost their support and left their land, the Peruvians were glad to be rid of him. Soon after, Peru unsuccessfully invaded Colombia, and Venezuela seceded from Colombia in 1829.

After two of his most trusted generals, Santander and Córdoba, rebelled against him, Bolívar wrote: "I am so worried. I shall go away to the country for several months, to a place where there are only Indians. I can't put up any longer with such ingratitude." Shortly before he died he scribbled on a piece of paper that he had wanted to be a king, adding in the margin, "but to accept a crown would stain my reputation. I prefer the glorious title of First Citizen of Colombia."

This valiant leader died of tuberculosis in 1830, as another military uprising was sweeping Colombia. Despite his accomplishments, Bolívar died a disappointed and broken man.

7

JORGE LUIS BORGES

"Let others boast of the pages they have written. I take pride in those I've read."

"He looks and talks like a drunk or a madman, but everything he says makes sense." This is how someone once described Jorge Luis Borges, the man often said to be the greatest living writer in Latin America.

Borges' genius as a writer has many forms of expression. He has won fame for his poetry, short stories, and essays. He considers himself an amateur philosopher, and his works reflect this. A man of many moods, he can be polite but restless, cheerful though impatient, warm yet elusive.

Descendant of an illustrious line of *criollos*, the names of his ancestors dot Argentine history. Borges was born on August 24, 1899, in Buenos Aires. His father was a lawyer and college teacher who brought up both Jorge and his sister Norah (now a well-known painter) to love books and art.

It was a sheltered life, however. Borges was tutored at home until the age of ten. He was physically frail, very nearsighted, and grew up to be shy and timid. Yet he always knew what he wanted to do with his life. "I never thought of myself as being anything but a writer," he has said. He spent long hours in his English grandmother's private library, reading books by Charles Dickens and other great British and American writers. This early reading gave rise to his admiration for the English language and his lifelong interest in the United States.

He wrote his first "book" when he was six years old. It was all of ten pages long! At the age of nine, he translated a story from English into Spanish.

In 1914 Borges went to Europe with his family. He remained there for several years, studying in Switzerland, England, and Spain. His first poem was published while he was in Spain.

By the time he returned to Argentina in 1921, Borges was eager to express his pride in his native land. He wrote poems about the Argentine pampas and the colorful *barrios* of Buenos Aires. He also began to write essays. In one of them—winner of a national prize—he called on his fellow writers to free the Spanish language from its antiquated rules and to create a new, living language without rhetoric. This in effect is what Borges has achieved in his poetry and prose. As a result, he has influenced an entire generation of Latin American writers.

Borges' father died in 1938. That year also marked two other changes in the writer's life. First, he obtained a job as a librarian (before this, he had lived off the family wealth). Also, he began to write the strange and fantastic short stories on which his later fame would be based. Although he has won world renown for his fiction, he has never written a novel.

His stories take place in remote times and places or imaginary worlds. Sometimes they occur in familiar settings that have been strangely twisted or transformed.

Readers are often confused by these tales, which have been described as games, puzzles, dreams, or nightmares. For example, in "The South," the hero must fight a duel. But neither the hero nor the reader is ever sure whether the duel is really taking place or whether it is just a dream.

In the 1940s, Borges' opposition to the Argentine dictator, Juan Perón, caused him to be fired from his library position, and his mother and sister were arrested. This did not stop him from writing and publishing, however. After the fall of Perón, in 1955, Borges was hailed as a national hero, awarded many prizes, and named director of the National Library of Argentina. By this time, his eyesight was failing, which forced him to do less writing and more teaching. In the 1960s, he spent two years as a lecturer in the United States, first at the University of Texas and then at Harvard.

"Texas was my first physical encounter with America," he recalled later. Yet, "in a sense, because of my reading, I had always been there. Though at times we fell into homesickness, I know now that my mother and I grew to love Texas."

Unlike many Latin American writers, Borges has always admired the United States. He believes in a free society and has spoken out against the philosophies of both the Nazis and the Communists. But he does not express his political views in his poetry and stories. "I have no message," he says. "I am simply a man of letters who turns his own confusion . . . into the forms of literature."

Borges did not marry until he was in his sixties. Before then, he had lived with his mother, who handled all his secretarial work until a few years ago and often accompanied him on his travels. Friends have hinted that there was a lost love in his youth. The woman he finally married had been a childhood friend.

Borges has been called "as frail as a shadow at nightfall" and "so mild in manner, so gentle and shy, that one could almost walk through him in the street." Yet he is a man of great courage. Like the Greek poet Homer, he is now completely blind. Many lesser men would have been crushed by blindness, but according to Borges, "Now the world is all inside me, and I see better, for I can see all the things I dream."

8

JULIA DE BURGOS

"Beyond my life, my words will carry a message."

Julia Constanza Burgos García was born on September 17, 1914, in a section called Santa Cruz, in Carolina, Puerto Rico. She was the first daughter born to Francisco Burgos Hans and his wife, Paula García. Six of Julia's twelve brothers and sisters died in early childhood.

The Burgos' house was a poor one with a thatched roof of palm leaves, but there was the warmth of a loving home within. Paula, the mother, kept a small garden nearby. She grew vegetables and grain to help feed the family, selling part of the produce to buy other food and clothing. Since she had no one with whom to leave her small daughter, Paula would take Julia along on her trips to the market, and it was then that the child began to recognize and love nature and the wonders that made up her world. Down by the river, while the washing was done in the stream, Julia and her sisters played in the grass and bathed in a pond they called The Deep Well.

The father, a strong, hard-working, and practical man, was nevertheless an inveterate dreamer. Of German extraction on his mother's side, Francisco Burgos took special pleasure in reading stories and adventures to his children. With his considerable knowledge of history and geography, he was able to help Julia with her studies. He liked to go horseback riding with his three eldest daughters—"all over the world," as the girls described their outings. The quaint safari would stop to doze off, munch on wild fruit, or sit and listen to the stories the father was always ready to tell his young traveling companions. Most of the time Julia rode a horse called *Nacional* and her father's was named *Rocinante*, after that of his favorite character, Don Quixote.

Life was simple for the Burgos family. Their world was limited to the countryside surrounding their house. But it seemed enormous and wondrous to Julia. Her eyes would discover the beauty of every wild flower, the living miracle of a bird's nest tucked away in a bush. Years later, reminiscing about her childhood, she confided, "I would cry disconsolately over the leaves of a *morivivi* because it would not awaken." *The morivivi* is a plant so sensitive that its leaves shrivel and die if someone touches it.

If Julia's childhood was poor in material wealth, it was rich in emotions and vital experiences. Unfortunately, it also abounded in sorrow. One by one, she saw six of her brothers and sisters die. The first time she saw her mother cry over the loss of one of her sons, Julia was devastated. She could not accept the fact that the dead child had to be buried. "Why don't they place him on a raft and cast him off on the river?" she asked her father repeatedly throughout the ceremony.

So that Julia could go to school, the family left their small country paradise and went to live in the town of Río Grande, not far from the mouth of the river Loiza, which was to play an important role in Julia's poetry. At school, Julia was a quick learner. She felt a tremendous need to know everything they could teach her. She helped her young brothers and sisters with their lessons and shared the housework with her mother. However, financial difficulties forced the family to return to Carolina. In desperation, Paula found a modest family that was willing to offer the in-

telligent young Julia a place to stay so she could continue her schooling. Doña Rosenda, the head of that household, was an educated woman who became very fond of Julia and gave her a great deal of understanding as well as a place in her home. Thus Julia was able to complete the eighth grade and graduate with honors.

When it came time for Julia to go on to high school, her family sold their little plot of land and moved again, this time to the town of Río Piedras. Julia again made their sacrifice worthwhile by graduating at the top of her class. She then enrolled in the University of Puerto Rico. It was as a college freshman that Julia joined the Puerto Rican Nationalist Party in their fight for freedom and political independence for the island. For the first time, Julia's young but passionate voice was heard in fiery patriotic poems.

One of Julia's first jobs took her to the town of Naranjito, in the heart of the Puerto Rican highland. Once again surrounded by mountains, open sky, rivers, and wilderness, the poet gave vent to her rapture, but this time her words were tempered by a new emotional maturity. From that happy balance came a collection entitled *Poemas exactos a mí misma,* which Julia gathered in a private edition in 1937. The most influential literary figures of Puerto Rico gave the book a warm welcome. One of them, the great poet Luis Lloréns Torres, suggested prophetically that, in time, the author would be best known by a shorter name, Julia de Burgos. That name became established in the Latin American literary scene in 1938, when Julia's first formally published book appeared with the title *Poema en veinte surcos.*

Not long after her first public success, Julia married a young artist, Rubén Rodríguez Beauchamp. He was a fine, sensitive man, but Julia was not destined for a quiet, lasting love.

In 1939 the Institute of Puerto Rican Literature awarded Julia the First Prize for Poetry for her book *Canción de la verdad sencilla.* She was showered with critical acclaim and public admiration, and with the money that went with the prize, she was able to relieve her family's impoverished situation. However, in October of that year, her mother died after a long and painful illness. A few months later Julia closed a recital of her poems at Puerto Rico's prestigious cultural society, the *Ateneo,* with *Elegía a mi madre,* a work equally rich in somber tones and tenderness. At the end of that recital, Julia met the man she was to love intensely but unhappily for the rest of her life. Social conventions precluded a permanent relationship. Nevertheless, trying to find some fleeting bliss, Julia followed her love to Cuba.

First in Havana and later in Santiago, Julia lived alone in modest rooms or humble apartments, asking only for a window to the sea, and waiting from day to day for an occasional visit from the man she loved. For a while she attended Havana University, where she met other intellectuals and resumed her literary work. It was in Cuba that she wrote her famous poems to her fickle love, a collection entitled *El mar y tú.* And there, in *Poemas para una muerte que puede ser la mía,* is the premonition of her own tragic end:

> *¡Dadme mi número, porque si no,*
> *me moriré después de muerta!*

Finally convinced that her love affair was hopeless, Julia moved to New York, where she was to live her last twelve years. She tried to follow the city's vibrant tempo. She worked at a variety of jobs. In time she married again. Her husband, Fernando Marín, offered peace and understanding, but Julia was unable to forget. She suffered one crisis of depression after another and tried to find relief in drinking. She had to be hospitalized twice. When she was discharged from a hospital on Welfare Island, she asked to be allowed to stay and help other patients. To them, her fellow sufferers, she dedicated a series of poems in English. One day she disappeared, never to be seen again.

On July 6, 1953, an unconscious woman was found lying on a Fifth Avenue sidewalk. There was no one to call; she carried no identification. They took her to Harlem Hospital, where she died, unknown. The body was taken to the city morgue, with only a number for identification. ("Give me my number, for if not. . . .")

After searching for Julia for five desperate days, her husband and friends finally were led to the morgue. There was a small but touching funeral in New York. In Puerto Rico, hundreds of friends and admirers awaited the arrival of her remains.

Julia de Burgos is buried in Carolina, her birthplace, close enough to the Río Grande de Loiza for the murmurs of the stream to reach those who visit her grave. She left a torrent of emotions and sensual force in her poetry.

9

CANTINFLAS

The Man Behind the Clown

To the moviegoer of Latin America, Cantinflas is a magic name. All a theatre has to do to fill the house to capacity is put his name on the marquee. The great comedian, Charlie Chaplin—with whom Cantinflas is often compared—once called the Mexican clown "the world's greatest comic artist."

Perhaps the secret of Cantinflas' success is the fact that he appeals to the downtrodden, common man in all of us. The character he plays is a nobody from the slums, a humble little fellow who through no fault of his own always gets in trouble with people in authority—the police, the ringmaster, the landlady, etc. He somehow manages to redeem himself and quite disarmingly turns the tables on the powerful. It is no wonder that the poor, the shy, and the powerless can identify with the plight—and the triumphs—of this character who is so much a part of themselves.

Cantinflas' real name is Mario Moreno. He was born in 1911 in Mexico City into a large and very poor family that lived in the city slums. His father was a postal clerk. Somehow Mario, who was bright and quick to learn, got himself admitted to medical school. He didn't last long as a medical student. Bored with academic life, he dropped out and worked at a variety of jobs. He was a busboy, a pool hall attendant, an assistant to a third-rate bullfighter, even a prizefighter! He remembers getting more lumps and cuts than money as a boxer, but he learned to sidestep fast, to duck, to dance, and most of all to "run quickly while seeming to stand still."

In 1928 he found himself working as a sort of singer and dancer in a *carpa*, a wandering tent show. One night, the emcee failed to show up and the manager grabbed Mario and shoved him on stage. "Say something!" the man told the astounded boy.

Frightened and confused, Mario started to talk nonsense, disconnected words in endless sentences. When the crowd began to laugh, Mario panicked and fled from the stage. The crowd thought this was part of the act and laughed even more. Valentina, the manager's daughter, caught him by the arm. "You're a hit!" she cried, pushing him back on stage. That same night after the show, the manager promoted Mario to full-time emcee, and Valentina offered to be his coach. Nine years later Mario Moreno and Valentina became man and wife.

Moreno's fame grew steadily. It was said that Mexico City's poor even pawned their shoes to buy tickets to see him perform. One night, a heckler in the audience—perhaps jealous of Mario's success despite his unassuming prose—shouted, *¡En la cantina tú inflas!* Mario liked the sound of that phrase, shortened it to Cantinflas, and adopted it as a stage name. Today the word has joined the Spanish language. Most modern dictionaries list the verb *cantinflar:* to speak nonsense, and the noun *cantinflada:* a long meaningless speech.

With the rise of the Mexican film industry in the early 1940s, Moreno, playing Cantinflas, became a movie star. In one of his hit films, Cantinflas was a lonely bum unjustly accused of murder. Trying to save himself, the desperate little man used his double talk in court. The judge and the jury became so confused that they began talking nonsense too, and the innocent bum was set free.

Moreno is short and slender, with high cheekbones, copper skin, a large mouth, and a flat nose. Even off-stage his eyes are full of sparkle and mischief, animating his mask-like Aztec face. He plays his famous role of Cantinflas dressed in striped baggy pants, an old-fashioned long-sleeved undershirt, and a squashed, nondescript hat. When thrown out of places where he is not wanted (he never seems to be wanted), he calls for his *gabardina*, his topcoat. Quickly, someone throws him a ragged strip of cloth, made of gabardine, which Mario drapes over his shoulder with great dignity as he is being kicked out. Made up with a tiny split mustache and foolish little eyebrows, the picture is complete: a nobody, a Great Clown.

Although he is a film idol in Latin America, Cantinflas is known in the United States for only one movie, *Around the World in Eighty Days,* which he made in 1956.

Mario Moreno, "Cantinflas", is one of the best-paid actors in the Spanish-speaking world. He owns several homes and a private airplane. But he is also known for his generosity. He gives away a percentage of his earnings to the poor and performs dozens of benefits each year. No legitimate Mexican cause that reaches him goes unattended. "I was born among the humble," he says. "I've never forgotten where I came from." Stories of his selflessness abound in Mexico. Once he bought a large ranch, hoping of course to make it into a profitable venture. But soon he began to sympathize with the farmhands who worked his land. He raised their wages 300 percent, built them modern houses and a medical dispensary, and had his own cattle slaughtered to provide meat for them and their families. Needless to say, the ranch didn't make much of a profit.

When asked about his success in making people laugh, he says, "I don't only try to make audiences laugh. I try to be *inside* the audience. Even if they are sad. I don't want them sad for long, though. I want them happy. That's why I try to make them laugh." Mario himself seldom laughs, on or off the stage. But those sparkling, mischievous eyes tell a different story. The clown *is* a happy man.

10

ALEJO CARPENTIER

A Man Who Chose His Destiny

Born in Havana, Cuba, in 1904, to a French architect father and a Russian physician mother, Alejo Carpentier grew up in an atmosphere of elegance and sophistication. His father awakened in him an early interest in architecture. Circumstances led him to practice journalism instead.

The press has often been the rostrum of Spanish-American writers with social concerns. There was serious unrest in Cuban politics, and Carpentier felt compelled to take part in the revolutionary movement. In 1924 he became the managing editor of *Carteles*, an illustrated liberal weekly of Havana.

In 1927 Carpentier was sentenced to seven months in prison for signing a revolutionary manifesto. His friend, the French poet

Robert Desnos, who was visiting Havana at the time, quickly got him a visa so that he could flee to France. In Paris, Alejo Carpentier was received with "the pomp and solemnity of a diplomatic envoy."

Carpentier expected to spend about two years in France, but he remained instead for eleven years. He felt at home among the intellectuals of Montmartre, especially the surrealists, who in his opinion exerted a great influence on contemporary Latin American culture.

The surrealists had a profound effect on his own thinking as well, although he could not adjust to all of their ideas. While this group of writers utilized "the marvelous" in an artificial fashion, Carpentier soon realized that in Latin America, lo maravilloso was an everyday element of nature and reality. Thus he came to the full realization that this *magic realism,* as he called it, was the expression of the Latin American soul.

Carpentier's years in Europe were only a prelude to his return to Latin America, where he tried to discover the magic realism that made it a world apart.

"I devoted myself to research, from the letters of Christopher Columbus to the works of the Inca Garcilaso de la Vega. I saw the American continent as a cloud that I longed to capture, for I sensed that this was going to be the essence of my work."

The modern Spanish-American novel was still undiscovered when Carpentier began to write. It was considered little more than a scenic regional sketch. Carpentier, however, was the first writer with a broad vision of the social, geographical, political, economic, and historical significance of the Latin American milieu.

Although his first novel, *Ecué-Yamba-O* (which in an African dialect means "praised be God"), was considered superficial and picturesque, it became a milestone in its own genre.

In *Tiento y diferencias,* a book of essays, Carpentier divided the continent into mountains, rivers, and valleys, indicating the spiritual characteristics of each. His purpose was to emphasize the specific and at the same time the typically regional quality in the life of Spanish America.

"A peculiar fact," he observed, "is that a single language, Spanish, serves as the instrument of communication among twenty different countries."

Alejo Carpentier has traveled widely and studied intensely. He has written on the most varied themes. His second novel, *El reino de este mundo,* published in 1949, is set in Haiti, whose historical background and present-day reality he probed in depth.

In his third novel, *Los pasos perdidos* (1964), the author can be identified with the principal figure, or protagonist. The book's theme is the return of a traveler who has become a stranger to himself. Knowing that he has lost his identity, he goes back to "pick up the scattered remnants." Some of the book's passages have an abstract quality that turns this psychological biography into a kind of myth. The book was written in exile in Venezuela, which in Carpentier's opinion is the "synthesis of the entire continent, with its enormous rivers, its immense mountains, its virgin forest."

Perhaps one of Carpentier's greatest novels is *El siglo de las luces,* (retitled *Explosion in a Cathedral* in its English version), a monumental work set in the Spanish and French colonies of the Antilles during the turmoil of the French Revolution and its aftermath. It was written in the late 1950s. Shortly after he completed it, Carpentier returned home to join the Castro revolution.

This work of Carpentier's seemed to foretell what was to occur in Cuba. Thus it is often studied from the viewpoint of his role as a spokesman and defender of the Cuban Revolution.

Convinced of the sacrifices required by the revolutionary task, he declared in his novel:

"Every revolutionary era has its martyrs. Under the guillotine or up against the wall, the massacre of innocents is an inevitable historical fact."

In one of his recent books, *El año '59* (first volume of a trilogy on the Cuban Revolution), he tried to show the results of collective labor. The work, however, was a literary failure in the West, considered by the critics to be only a collection of facts.

Nevertheless, Carpentier is satisfied with his social mission, even when in order to fulfill it he has had to sacrifice some of the popularity he achieved in the 1940s. He is, however, counted among the writers of the Latin American literary "boom" that included Vargas Llosa, García Márquez, Asturias, Rulfo, Cortázar, and others. Today he is his country's cultural attaché at its embassy in France and its chief Cuban delegate to UNESCO.

11

PABLO CASALS

*". . . asking each one to put the purity
of his art at the service of mankind . . ."*

In the summer of 1973, a few months before his death at the age of ninety-six, Pablo Casals gave a free concert in New York's Central Park.

"What can I say to you?" the world's greatest cellist asked the crowd. "I am perhaps the oldest musician in the world. I am an old man, but in many senses I am also a very young man. And this is what I want you to be, young, young all your life, and to say things to the world that are true.

"Goodness, love . . . . This is the real world," he added. "Let us have love, love and peace. I love you. Thank you."

These remarks show why Casals was such a remarkable human being. His sensitivity, his love of humanity, his devotion to music, and his youthful spirit made him one of the most highly admired men in the world.

Casals was born in 1876 in Vendrell, Spain, where his father was the town organist. "From my earliest days," he said, "music was for me a natural element, an activity as natural as breathing." He learned to carry a tune even before he could speak clearly. By the age of five, he was a singer in the church choir. His father taught him to play the piano, violin, and organ. When he was eight years old, he even began to substitute for his father as church organist.

Casals first heard a cello at the age of ten. He became so excited that his father built him a makeshift cello, with a gourd for a sounding board. Soon after this, he went to study the cello at the Barcelona School of Music. Casals' father had opposed this, wanting him to become a carpenter, but Pablo's mother disagreed and took him to Barcelona herself. To support himself, he played in the evenings at a well-known café.

Casals' greatest artistic inspiration came from the music of Johann Sebastian Bach, the eighteenth-century German composer. He first came upon Bach's cello suites while visiting a music shop with his father.

"I forgot entirely the reason of my visit to the shop and could only stare at and hear this music which nobody had told me about," he said years later. "Sometimes even now when I look at the covers of that old music, I again see the inside of that musty shop with its faint smell of the sea.

"I took the suites home and read and reread them. For twelve years after that, I studied and worked at them every day. I was nearly twenty-five before I had the courage to play one of them in public."

His professional breakthrough came in 1899, just before his twenty-third birthday. He arrived in Paris with a letter of introduction to the famous conductor, Charles Lamoureux. The conductor was quite unfriendly at first, but then the young cellist began to play. With the first notes, Lamoureux rose from his desk and stood facing Casals until he finished playing. Lamoureux then hugged him and said, "My boy, you are one of the chosen."

Casals became a sensation in Paris. Shortly after, he played in London for Queen Victoria. He made his New York debut in 1904, and for the next twenty years he toured the major cities of the Western world, winning the critics' praise everywhere.

After World War I he returned to Spain, where he began to work actively for the poor. For example, he founded the Workingman's Concert Association in Barcelona, which gave the city's underprivileged a chance to hear concerts and set up their own musical groups.

In the 1930s Casals was a strong supporter of the Spanish Republic during the Civil War. When Barcelona fell to Franco's army, Casals fled to France. For the rest of his life, he refused to live or perform in Spain.

So opposed was Casals to all totalitarian governments that he turned down offers to visit both Nazi Germany and Communist Russia. He said he could not separate his beliefs as a human being from his work as a musician.

After World War II, Casals halted his concert career for several years in protest of the Allies' unwillingness to help overthrow Franco. In 1951, however, he met the great missionary doctor, Albert Schweitzer, who urged him to return to the concert stage. "It is better to create than to protest," Dr. Schweitzer said. "Why not do both? Why not create *and* protest?"

Casals thought seriously about this advice and he soon began to perform again. In 1958 he played at the United Nations to call world attention to the danger of nuclear war. He launched a one-man musical peace mission which he carried to concert halls throughout the world.

"As a man," he said in 1962, "my first obligation is toward the welfare of my fellow men. I will endeavor to meet that obligation through music, the means which God has given me, since it transcends language, politics, and national boundaries."

Casals' mother was a native of Puerto Rico, and in 1956 he moved to the beautiful tropical island. It remained his home for the rest of his life. At the age of eighty, he married Marta Montañez, one of his cello students, who was then twenty-one. Casals' earlier marriages had ended in divorce, but he found happiness with this young Puerto Rican woman. "Martita is the marvel of my world," he once said, "and each day I find some new wonder in her. I am aware that I am no longer exactly a youth, but if I speak of her in words perhaps expected of young lovers, it is because that is how I feel about her."

If there is a key to Casals' life, perhaps it was his great capacity for joy, love, and sorrow. A cello student, practicing a Bach suite, once said to him, "I think it goes like this."

"Don't think," replied the master. "It is better to *feel*."

12

MIGUEL DE CERVANTES SAAVEDRA

"Either this man is crazy, or he is reading Don Quijote."–Philip II

If the work of Miguel de Cervantes Saavedra represents a milestone in the history of Spanish literature, the story of his life can be considered as a great unwritten novel. Cervantes is revered as the supreme innovative genius of Spanish literature. *Don Quijote de La Mancha,* his immortal work, is still regarded by many as one of the world's greatest novels. It has been the most widely read book in many languages, second only to the Bible.

The fourth of seven children and the second son, Miguel de Cervantes was born September 29, 1547, in Alcalá de Henares, a small town near Madrid. His father, Rodrigo de Cervantes, studied law and served as a magistrate in various parts of Spain, although he made his living as an itinerant surgeon. His mother's name was Leonor Cortinas.

Between the years 1552 and 1553, Rodrigo moved his family to Valladolid and was jailed there for indebtedness. After his release in 1561, he took his family to Madrid, where Philip II had established the capital.

From his earliest days, Miguel showed a passion for reading. His voracity for the printed word was so great that he would pick up what papers he found in the street in order to read them.

In 1569 Cervantes published his first known work in a book of elegies to Isabel de Valois, Philip II's third wife, who died in 1568. The early death of the beautiful princess was mourned by the whole country. The publisher, Juan López de Hoyos, a well-known professor of Latin, included an elegy by Cervantes in the book and referred to him repeatedly as "my beloved disciple."

In 1569 Cervantes joined the Spanish army departing for Naples under the command of Don Juan of Austria, half-brother of Philip II. Don Juan arrived on the ninth of August and three weeks later he was in active service. The Armada consisted of 208 galleys, 7 galleons, and 24 schooners. It was the world's largest fleet, numbering 26,000 men.

On October 7, 1571, there took place at the entrance to the Bay of Corinth what in the words of Cervantes was "the greatest event that generations past or present have witnessed," the battle of Lepanto. *La Marquesa,* the vessel in which he sailed, was in the center of the action, and no one surpassed Cervantes in valor. Suffering from fever, he refused to leave his battle station and go below. He chose the most exposed position. He was wounded twice in the chest and a third volley maimed his left hand "for the greater glory of the right."

Cervantes was proud of his role in that battle, which won him the nickname of "the one-handed man of Lepanto." He returned to Spain with his brother Rodrigo, who also had joined the combat troops. The galley *El Sol,* in which they traveled, was attacked by Turkish corsairs, who took the brothers to Algeria as slaves. Cervantes spent five years in captivity despite several escape attempts and his family's efforts to ransom him. His freedom was finally paid for by the Catholic Brothers of the Trinitarian Order.

After his return to Spain, Cervantes was married to Catalina de Salazar y Palacios who was eighteen years his junior. Her parents did not look favorably upon the match, but they gave her a dowry of several vineyards, an orchard, some furniture, four beehives, forty-five hens and chickens, and one rooster.

Prior to his childless marriage to Catalina, Miguel had had one daughter by Isabel de Saavedra and another by Ana Franca de Rojas. The memory of Isabel was to haunt him until the end of his life.

The death of his father in 1585 greatly increased Cervantes' responsibilities. He had to support his sisters and one niece. This forced him to seek a new source of income. Driven by necessity, he sold the publication rights to his work, *La Galatea*, for 1,336 reales, which was not a large sum.

In 1587 he went to Seville to seek employment as a supplier to the Spanish fleet. This job marked a fifteen-year absence from his literary career. He was excommunicated for excessive zealousness in complying with his duty to the Spanish navy—he had confiscated grain supplies that belonged to the Cathedral of Seville and Ecija! This opened for Cervantes a period of mishaps and economic difficulties in his new post as chief petty officer of the navy, in which he remained after the defeat of the Spanish fleet.

In May 1590, Cervantes requested a transfer to a vacant post in the Indies, but the Council of the Indies rejected his application, and he had to continue working as a petty officer in Seville. His troubles increased with the constant struggle to collect his twelve reales a day which were later reduced to ten reales. In November he was forced to take out a loan to buy a suit of clothes, and in August of the following year he was accused of a deficit in the accounts of the navy, a debt for which he had to answer.

In September 1592, his fondness for the theatre led him to sign a contract with Rodrigo Osorio of Seville to write six plays at six ducats each, on the condition that they be staged twenty days after the manuscript was delivered; payment would be deferred if in Osorio's opinion the plays were not "the best works presented in Spain." The agreement was a failure. To add to his misfortunes, Cervantes was jailed in Ecija for fifteen days for illegal collection of payments. Squabbles with the tribunal of the Treasury further complicated his situation.

In 1594 his salary was raised to sixteen reales a day. During his rare moments of peace he managed to write. In May 1595, he won the first prize—three silver spoons—for a poetic composition he had sent to a contest in Zaragoza. In mid-1596 Cervantes entrusted 7,400 reales to a banker in Seville to be paid to the Treasury in Madrid. The banker disappeared and the money could not be recovered until January 1597. Less than a year later Cervantes was sentenced to three months in jail for failing to present himself in Madrid within twenty days. With this incident his official employment seemed to have ended, although in 1599 and 1601 the government continued to summon him to appear and clear up his accounts in Madrid. Still in Seville, meanwhile, Cervantes had to resort to moneylenders in order to feed and clothe himself.

Nothing is known of Cervantes' whereabouts between 1600 and 1603. It is possible that he was reunited with his wife Catalina in a peaceful corner of Esquivias writing his *Don Quijote*. This great novel was originally conceived as a parody of the romances of chivalry, which for a century had been exerting a hypnotic attraction on readers of every social class.

When Cervantes reappeared in Madrid in 1604, it was to help in the publication of his work: *El ingenioso hidalgo Don Quijote de La Mancha,* which came out in Madrid in January 1605.

Although his earlier works had not enjoyed great success, *Don Quijote* aroused an enthusiasm never seen in Spain. The profound philosophy and healthy humor of its characters captured the attention of all; young and old, rich and poor, nobleman and commoner. Even the king himself was aware of the book's popularity, as depicted in this incident:

From the terrace of his palace, Philip II saw a young student seated in a nearby garden, reading a book. Hearing the young man's guffaws, the king could not contain himself. "Either that man is crazy or he is reading *Don Quijote!*" he said to his aide.

Weeks after the first authorized edition of the *Quijote* was published, three fraudulent editions appeared in Lisbon. A second edition, revised and authorized by the author, was again published in Madrid. Cervantes obtained publication rights in Lisbon and Aragón. Two more editions appeared in Valencia that same year. The first English edition of the *Quijote,* translated by Thomas Shelton, was dated 1612.

In 1613 Cervantes' *Novelas ejemplares* were published in Madrid, dedicated to the Count of Lemos to whom Cervantes could finally turn for economic support. In 1614 he published *Viaje al Parnaso* and in 1615 *Ocho comedias y ocho entremeses nuevos.*

Cervantes had promised to write a *segunda parte* or continuation of *Don Quijote.* He was working on chapter 59 when he learned that in 1614 a phony edition entitled *Segunda parte de El Quijote* had been published in Tarragona by Alonso Fernández de Avellaneda. The spurious book did not lack a great sense of humor, but what left Cervantes indignant was the insolent prologue in which the author attributed to Cervantes innumerable physical and moral defects.

Hurriedly, Cervantes finished his *segunda parte* and unleashed his rancor against Avellaneda in the text of the book, which appeared in Madrid at the end of 1615 and whose success was such, that it was reprinted immediately in Brussels, Valencia, and Lisbon. The first French translation appeared in 1618, two years after Cervantes' death.

Cervantes undertook new projects with tremendous zeal, realizing that he did not have long to live. He did not survive to see his last work published, *Los trabajos de Persiles y Sigismunda*. Its first edition, published in 1617, was followed by eight others in two years, two French translations in 1618, and an English translation a year later.

Miguel de Cervantes Saavedra died at his home on Calle León in Madrid, April 23, 1616. He was buried in the Monastery of La Trinidad. No stone marks his grave. He left no known will. Spanish literature, magnificently enriched by his genius, was his only heir.

13

CARLOS CHÁVEZ

Giant of Mexican Music

Take the finest European musical traditions, mix in the dramatic rhythms of the New World, add the vitality of the Nahuatl Indian mixed with Spanish blood, shake with a measure of genius, and you get Carlos Chávez, the composer and conductor who changed the course of Mexican music and enriched the musical legacy of the world.

Maestro Chávez was born in Mexico City on June 13, 1899, the seventh child in a musical family. His mother used to lull him to sleep by playing Mozart and Beethoven softly on the piano. Carlos himself began taking piano lessons from his brother at the age of ten. In a household of musicians, talent like his was bound to be discovered early, and soon the promising teenager was sent to study with two of Mexico's great composers, Manuel Ponce and Pedro Ogazón.

Carlos composed his first serious pieces at the age of sixteen, most of them based on folkloric themes. However, between his seventeenth and eighteenth years, he fell totally under the influence of the European romantic classical traditions in which he had been trained. It was then that he composed his first major works, including a symphony and a sonata.

By 1920, European composers were at the peak of their rebellion against romanticism and neoclassicism. The movement fascinated the young Mexican composer who organized a string quartet to play the music of "rebels" like Erik Satie and Igor Stravinsky.

At the age of twenty-two, Chávez went to Europe to immerse himself in the latest developments in twentieth-century music. From Europe he went to New York, where some of Stravinsky's pupils—Gershwin among them—were establishing "modern music" even in popular performances.

After two years of hard work in the United States, Carlos Chávez returned home. He married a young Mexican pianist (today the mother of his three children), introduced European and American modern music to Mexican audiences, and initiated a process that eventually was to bring Mexican music to the world.

Yearning to rediscover himself as a composer through his country's native music, Chávez embarked on a pilgrimage that took him to remote villages deep in the jungles and high mountains of his land. He lived with the Indians, learning their language, their musical traditions, and their instruments. He felt the need to relate his compositions to the daily life and struggles, the history, and the myths of his people. Among the pieces which followed that determination was *Los cuatro soles,* with a score based on Aztec themes and scales hitherto little known to concert audiences. The departure not only created new respect for native Indian culture, it also spurred the interest of other young innovative composers in the musical lore of their land.

Chávez's feeling for the life of the common people of Mexico went beyond the rural scene. He was deeply moved by the urban struggles of daily life in the capital. From those observations came his ballet *Horsepower,* inspired by the machine age. The work was premiered in 1930, conducted by Leopold Stokowski, with costumes and scenery designed by Mexico's great painter, Diego Rivera. Having found a parallel between so-called "primitive music" and machine sound, Chávez developed a simultaneous interest in both.

Chávez stripped his music of all unnecessary adornments. For that reason his compositions are called linear rather than harmonic. He gets clean, definite sounds from gourds, clavés, maracas, bongos, and other types of native drums. Rather than seek tonal harmony in conventional instrumentation, he achieves an impact through intricate rhythm patterns that contrast with each other. Because his style depends greatly on native instruments, it was first called "neoprimitive." American composer Aaron Copland has described the music of his long-time friend Chávez as "stoic, stark, somber, like an Orozco painting," a very vivid description.

Flattered and secure as Chávez was with his first successes in "neoprimitive" inventions, he cautioned faddists against creating without a firm base of originality, just to be different or sensational. "Nothing is totally new," he said. "Each work, however new it appears, has many antecedents. Bach would not be Bach if Vivaldi and Buxtehude had not lived before him." To that he added his belief in total immersion in the creative process. "Concentration is inspiration," he said. "You must be completely overtaken by your work and your subject. Only then do all our influences and experience come up to surface."

In 1928 Chávez established the Symphony Orchestra of Mexico and took over the direction of the National Conservatory of Music. He introduced native instruments in the former and radically changed the curriculum of the latter—both against the expected opposition of diehard traditionalists. Chávez continued to pursue his dreams and plans under a motto that might read, "Respect for the old, love and attention for the new." It is curious that some of his best works date from the years of strife and toil he spent between the podium, the classroom, and his composing table; works like his *Sinfonía Antígona*, composed in 1933; *Sinfonía India* 1935-36; *La Paloma azul*, a cantata (composition for chorus and symphony orchestra) premiered in 1940.

Since then Chávez has enjoyed international acclaim. He has appeared as guest conductor with almost every major symphony in the West; his works are recorded and performed everywhere. In 1960 the United States made him an honorary member of the National Institute of Arts and Letters. The Mexican government commissioned him to write the ceremonial music for the Olympic Games of 1968, which took place in Mexico City.

Always the harbinger, in recent years Chávez has been interested in the possibility of new musical instruments that could be developed from the latest electronic devices at Bell Telephone Laboratories. He divides his time between his two beloved cities, Mexico and New York.

Carlos Chávez is often called a giant. He is, in more ways than one. His formerly jet-black hair today is almost white, but it still crowns an imposing erect figure that towers over most people. Artists have no trouble spotting him in the audience when they want the composer to stand up and take a bow. He is likely to be wearing a turtleneck sweater rather than a shirt and tie, for "the giant" is as informal as he is chivalrous. One invariably sees him at rehearsals in an oversized sweatshirt, his deep dark eyes giving as many cues as the elegant swaying of his arms.

It is a joy to hear a Chávez-led symphony orchestra playing a baroque piece in all its glory only to change the tempo and pulse in the next number, and fill the hall with something exotic and exciting that speaks of earth, humanity, and *now*. "Respect for the old, love and attention for the new."

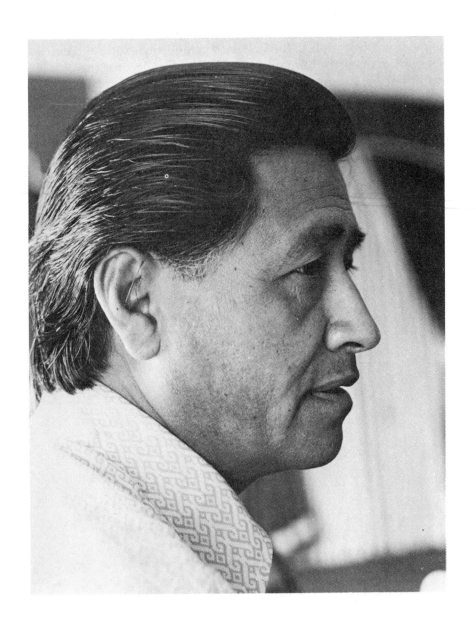

14

CÉSAR CHÁVEZ

Champion of the Farm Workers

César Chávez was born poor and is poor today. His voice is soft and his manner is gentle, but he has a tremendous inner strength and vitality. His life has been devoted to organizing one of the most downtrodden groups in America, the migrant farm workers. Through Chávez's untiring efforts, the world has become acutely aware of the migrant's plight.

Chávez was born in 1927 on a small farm near Yuma, Arizona. His parents went bankrupt during the Depression, and the county government evicted them from their farm for nonpayment of taxes. When César was ten, the family moved to California, where they became migrant workers.

Like all migrants, they had to move frequently to follow the crops. César grew up in a series of labor camps. He lived in tar-paper shacks and often hid under bridges to avoid the cold and rain. By the time he had reached the seventh grade, César had attended over thirty schools. This instability had a negative effect on him. Although he was highly intelligent, he did not learn to read and write well. His parents were too poor to send him to high school, so César's seventh year was his last year of formal education.

As he grew up, César learned about prejudice and the suffering that it breeds. Many of the schools that he attended were segregated; the Spanish-American children were separated from the Anglo children. He often saw signs in storefronts that read, "No Dogs or Mexicans Allowed." The law helped to enforce segregation. Once, the police physically removed him from the white section of a movie theater. He was deeply wounded by these incidents and knew that he would fight someday to end this intolerance.

During World War II, Chávez joined the navy. After the war, he returned to migrant work in California. There he met and married Helen Fabela, whose father had been a colonel under Pancho Villa. They now have eight children.

In the 1950s, Chávez worked for an antipoverty program. The job was a good one, but he never forgot the plight of his people. He thought long and hard about becoming a union organizer. He remembered that when he was a child, many men had tried, but failed to organize the migrants.

Why had these attempts to form a union failed? César soon found out. Migrant workers moved from place to place too frequently. They were too poor to pay union dues and survive without work during a strike. Also, the state and federal laws that protected the rights of other types of workers did not protect them.

In spite of these overwhelming difficulties, Chávez was determined to succeed. In 1962 he moved his family to Delano, California. His wife took a job picking grapes, while he spent all his energy attempting to organize the migrants. Chávez drove his 1953 Mercury through the valley, talking to workers when their bosses were not around. His plan succeeded. By the beginning of 1965, he had miraculously persuaded about 1,000 people—most of whom were grape pickers—to join the United Farm Workers union.

That year, a group of Filipino workers in the vineyards decided to go on strike. Chávez and his union voted to join them. The Filipino workers had only asked for a wage increase to $1.40 an hour. Chávez's union supported this request, but it also wanted paid vacations and holidays, better housing, and toilets in the fields.

Five thousand workers went on strike. The bosses refused to give in, but they knew that if the grapes were not picked, the crop would be lost. Strikebreakers were hired to pick the grapes, and the strike dragged on for months. Many people became aware of the hardships of the migrants. The union began to draw strong support from churches, college students, and other unions. These groups not only sent food, clothing, and money, but they also joined the workers on picket lines.

The union then organized a nationwide boycott of California grapes. Throughout the United States, shoppers refused to buy grapes. The farm workers also organized large demonstrations. In 1966 Chávez led a 300-mile march to the state capitol in Sacramento. Public opinion finally pressured the growers into signing contracts that granted the workers $1.75 an hour. The growers later tried to back out of their agreement, outraging the workers. The strike continued and, contrary to Chávez's instructions, violence broke out on the picket lines.

Chávez, a religious, nonviolent man, decided to fast as an act of both protest and prayer. In the spring of 1968, he fasted for twenty-five days. He survived on a little bouillon, grapefruit juice, and water. At the end of his fast, Chávez had lost forty pounds and had to be carried to a mass of thanksgiving in Delano Park. Four thousand of his followers listened to him say: "I am convinced that the truest act of courage, the strongest act of manliness, is to sacrifice ourselves for others, in a totally nonviolent struggle for justice. To be a man is to suffer for others. God help us to be men."

Chávez was to suffer a great deal. He had back problems which resulted in physical deformity. One of his legs and one side of his pelvis is smaller than the other. The fast aggravated this back condition and left him bedridden. He finally had to be hospitalized, and his condition was diagnosed as a ruptured spinal disc.

Early in 1969, Senator Edward Kennedy sent Dr. Janet Travell at his own expense to treat Chávez in the hospital. Dr. Travell was the back specialist who had helped John Kennedy. She realized that Chávez's problem was not spinal in origin, but was the result of a muscular breakdown in his back. She gave him excellent care and suggested that his back would improve if he used a rocking chair. Chávez gradually felt stronger and eventually was able to leave his bed.

When Chávez came out of the hospital, he had a tremendous amount of work to accomplish. Eleven grape growers had already signed contracts with the union. The contracts provided the workers with $2.25 an hour and other benefits, but they only affected a few thousand farm workers. More than 300,000 still needed help!

In the early 1970s new troubles threatened the union. The growers made an agreement with the Teamsters' Union, a rival of Chávez's United Farm Workers. The Teamsters were to organize in the UFW local's areas, and the growers would then sign contracts with the Teamster locals. At first, this arrangement seemed to work, but the Teamsters tried to force the workers to join them. Many workers were beaten, including women, and two people were murdered. Shocked and outraged, the rest of the labor movement turned its support to Chávez's union.

Today, the United Farm Workers continue their fight. Their difficult task of organizing hundreds of thousands of workers is complicated by the fact that new types of farm machinery are putting many of them out of work. When asked if he was willing to compromise his position, Chávez said, "It's a nonviolent fight to the death. They destroy our union or we conquer them. There's no turning back now. If you win nonviolently, then you have a double victory. You have not only won your fight, but you remain free."

In spite of all he has endured—physical deprivation, persecution, beatings, jailings, and constant threats against his life—he has no fear of death and maintains a keen sense of humor about life. "No one accepts death," he has said, "but what is the alternative? . . . You're really too busy to think of it."

Chávez has indeed been very busy with life. It is not hard to understand why many consider him to be "one of the heroic figures of our time." Chávez has spoken out to the poor and underprivileged, but it is not only the poor who have listened to him. During the 1965 UFW grape strike, he attracted national and international support. Now, more than 300 contracts have been won for his people, but his task is far from complete.

César Chávez has gone on working for the self-respect and the courage his people need to triumph over unfair and intolerable conditions. In the process, he continues to make people everywhere aware of the needs of humanity.

15

ROBERTO CLEMENTE

"I don't need to be loved.
I just wish it would happen."

Roberto Clemente won fame for himself and his native Puerto Rico as a great baseball player. A major-league manager once called him "a one-man team. . .one of the most amazing athletes of all time."

But Clemente was more than a great ballplayer. He was also a deeply compassionate man who cared about other people and believed in being of service to them. In fact, he was on his way to Nicaragua to aid the victims of an earthquake when he was killed in a plane crash on December 31, 1972.

Roberto Clemente was born in Puerto Rico in 1934. His father was a foreman on a large sugar plantation and ran a grocery store for the sugar workers.

Roberto's parents wanted him to have a better life than they had known. "They worked like racehorses for me," he once told a reporter.

Clemente was a softball player when, at the age of seventeen, he was noticed by the owner of a local professional baseball team. He played with this team for three years; in his last year, he batted .356. The Brooklyn Dodgers signed him for a $10,000 bonus, more than they had ever paid to a Hispanic player.

Before the Dodgers could bring him to the major leagues, however, he was acquired in a special draft by the Pittsburgh Pirates. This turned out to be the best thing the Pirates had ever done. They had finished last in the National League in 1954, but with Roberto Clemente they slowly became a winning team.

During his first five years with the Pirates, Clemente did not do well. He was often moody and bitter and felt that he was misunderstood. But in his sixth season he suddenly caught fire and scored a very high batting average. During his career, he led the National League in batting three times. On September 30, 1972, he became the eleventh player in major league history to reach the 3,000 hit mark.

In 1967, *Sport* magazine asked the major league managers who they thought was the best baseball player. Almost half named Clemente.

When asked about Clemente in 1971, Pittsburgh third baseman José Pagán said: "To me, Roberto is the most complete player in the game. He hits, he fields, he throws well, he's a smart player . . . and he hustles all the time."

Clemente led the Pirates in 1971 to victory over the Baltimore Orioles in the World Series, four games to three. This gave him his greatest satisfaction, and a sportswriter said, "The wounded pride of Roberto Clemente is almost healed. Now he can rest and his brown eyes can twinkle."

After the 1971 Series, Clemente decided to use his money to begin building what he had dreamed of for thirteen years: a "sports city" for the youth of Puerto Rico. He saw this as a way to keep young people from experimenting with drugs. "They spend millions of dollars for drug control in Puerto Rico," he said, "but they attack the problem after it is there. Why not attack it before it starts?" If a boy were really interested in sports, Roberto felt he would not turn to drugs. This was not hollow talk for Clemente was serious about helping others. "Anyone who has the opportunity to serve his country or his island and doesn't, God should punish him."

Yet in spite of his fame, he was very modest. The people of Río Piedras, Puerto Rico, where he lived during the off-season, wanted him to run for mayor, but he declined. He did not want to be elected simply because of his popularity.

Clemente was 5'11" and weighed 180 pounds. On the field he used a waist-high "basket" catch so that he could follow the ball with his eyes right into the glove.

Clemente helped the other members of his team in a very special way. "Basically, it was his presence," one player remembers. "He inspired us to give nothing less than our best. He really had fun in the club house. A lot of the time one guy can mean a lot to you."

When the tragic earthquake hit Managua, Nicaragua, in 1972, Clemente immediately helped form a committee to aid the hungry and the homeless. He loaded an airplane with food and supplies and took off from the San Juan airport. The plane crashed into the sea only a mile from San Juan. Puerto Ricans, both on the island and in the United States, went into mourning for the man they had loved and admired. It was the death of a hero.

In a special election held in January 1973, Roberto Clemente was voted into baseball's Hall of Fame. He was the second player in history—the first was Lou Gehrig—to be admitted in this way. Clemente's widow, Vera, said about this great honor: "This is Roberto's last triumph. If he were here now, he would dedicate this honor to the people of Puerto Rico and to people all over the United States."

16

RUBÉN DARÍO

Bridge Between Two Literary Eras

His life was one of hardship and anguish, yet his poetry is among the most beautiful in the Spanish language. Modernism, a major literary school of the late nineteenth century, began and ended with him. So great was Rubén Darío's influence that in every literary trend from his time to the present, something of his magic can be felt.

Félix Rubén García Sarmiento was born January 18, 1867, in a humble household in Metapa, Nicaragua. The pseudonym Darío, by which he would be known, came from an ancestor of local fame. He was reared by relatives who felt no affection for him and disliked his precocious ways. By the time he was thirteen, he was already writing poems and essays of a high quality. They called him the poet child. At the age of fourteen, he was honored by the president of Guatemala in the Presidential Palace with a reception attended by some of the outstanding intellectual figures of his country.

At age eighteen he was appointed to his first diplomatic mission in Paris. This was to be the beginning of a long career as diplomatic representative, cultural attaché, press correspondent, and intellectual ambassador of Nicaragua.

In Paris, Rubén Darío frequented literary circles and met the fashionable authors of the day. He came under the influence of the symbolist poets and the Parnassians*—Valery, Mallarmé, etc. He returned to America brimming with new ideas.

In 1888 in Chile, he published his first book, *Azul*. It was a literary event of tremendous importance in the Spanish-speaking world. *Azul* is a volume of poetry and prose, strongly influenced by the French Parnassians, but nevertheless different and unique.

Darío's words were utilized in such an innovative way, it seemed as if they were being used for the first time. There was an element of surprise and fascination in his metaphors. It was at this time that the young Darío proclaimed to the world his first aesthetic manifesto, "Words must paint the color of a sound, the aroma of a star; they must capture the heart of the matter."

From Chile, Rubén Darío went to Buenos Aires as honorary consul of Colombia. Upon returning to Central America in 1889, he married a Costa Rican woman, Rafaelita Contreras. They went to Spain, where they lived beautiful yet bitter days of severe economic hardship. The Spanish poets received Darío as a hero, a demigod poet. He was the center of attention in the literary salons. But his economic circumstances did not match his intellectual fame. Rubén Darío had to return to his country, filled with both glory and bitterness.

Rafaelita, his wife, the "Stella" of his poems, died six months later. Their only son was adopted by his maternal grandfather and given the name Rubén Darío Contreras. Darío's father-in-law accused him

---

*A school of French poets who stressed metrical perfection and rejected personal emotion as a theme.

of being responsible for the death of Rafaelita and incapable of caring for the boy.

In a severe state of depression, the poet went to Paris. He suffered horrible nightmares and began to drink heavily. In the midst of his hallucinations, he remembered a peasant girl, whom he had seen while walking one afternoon with the writer, Valle-Inclán, on the outskirts of Madrid. Her name was Francisca Sánchez and she was to play an important role in Darío's life, giving him fourteen years of selfless love. The poet referred to her in his verses as *"lazarillo de Dios en mi camino"* and in his periods of anguish he called to her, *"Francisca Sánchez, acompáñame."*

Rubén Darío returned to Madrid to seek out his friends and Francisca. He felt strong again and continued to be the soul and guiding spirit of new literary trends. In 1893 he published his *Prosas profanas*, a book that weaves together a wealth of rhythm, beauty, and color. In it, Darío says that, *"el placer es un juego y por lo mismo, un ritual que incluye dolor y sacrificio."*

Darío searched for "the beauty that is more beautiful than beauty itself" and only found the "word that escapes." It was the same frustration felt by other poets of that time, from Mallarmé to Baudelaire; a frustration that often leads to irony or silence.

Darío's influence continued to be felt by the Hispanic writers of his literary generation, among them poets from both Spain and Latin America. His poetry was virile, sensual, powerful; the work of a romantic who was also a Parnassian and a symbolist.

Plagued by a lack of funds, embittered by the disloyalty of some who called themselves friends only to exploit him, Darío returned to Nicaragua. Again he began to drink heavily. A beautiful but scheming woman, Rosario Murillo, forced him to marry her, while all she wanted was "the glory of his fame."

Because of Rosario—*"la garza morena"* of his verses—the poet was unable to return to Spain to fulfill a promise of marriage to Francisca Sánchez. But he recalled his "sweet companion," to whom he wrote short letters filled with tenderness. In them he called her "mi tataya, conejita, hijita." He never saw the first daughter of his love with Francisca. The child, Carmencita, died at an early age.

Darío's second marriage was even more tragic than his first. Rosario Murillo constantly blamed him for their lack of money, for his weakness for alcohol, for his moral crises. She finally abandoned him and went off with a lover.

Again Darío fell into deep despair and looked for a way to return to Paris. The year was 1903. Francisca Sánchez came to the poet's side. She looked after him and pampered him. Sitting quietly at his side, she copied the words he taught her and learned to write correctly. From this encounter another son was born, Rubén Darío Sánchez. His father dedicated a poem to him in which he called him *Phocás, el campesino*. The child died of pneumonia at a very early age.

In 1906, Rubén went to New York. There he met José Martí, the Cuban poet. He spent some time there working as a librarian, café waiter, and book salesman. From there he wrote sweet letters to Francisca. He sent her money whenever he could. In one of his letters he said, *"Sé siempre buena y piensa en ser inteligente."* From his last reunion with Francisca, another son was born and again given the poet's name. His father affectionately called him *el Guicho*. Rubén loved the child deeply. He returned to Paris, where he spent a long time with Francisca and their son.

The publication of *Cantos de vida y esperanza* revived Darío's fame. His friends found him and invited him to go drinking. Some exploited his lack of will power. The publishers failed to pay him and the newspapers he worked for paid him very little.

In 1914 Darío's health began to fail. Europe was at war. By 1915 his situation was critical. A group of poets from the Americas tried to offer him a series of lectures throughout South America and the Antilles, but the project failed. The poet arrived in New York gravely ill. He was hospitalized and underwent a liver operation. His economic situation continued to be critical. While convalescing, he traveled to Guatemala, and from there he returned to his native Nicaragua.

On February 16, 1916, Darío, one of the greatest poets of the Americas, died in his native town. He had named his last son, Rubén Darío Sánchez, *el Guicho*, heir to his literary rights, but the inheritance was given over to his legitimate son, Rubén Darío Contreras.

The poet is buried in the magnificent Cathedral of León, Nicaragua. "Over his tomb they have placed a horrible marble lion, like the kind the wealthy put in front of their homes," said Federico García Lorca, the Spanish poet. And again, speaking of Darío's tomb, Pablo Neruda, the Chilean poet, referred to the "lion without stars, for he [Darío] who was the creator of stars."

"A Spaniard from America and an American in Spain"—that is how Rubén Darío regarded himself. America and Spain still honor his memory.

17

JUAN PABLO DUARTE

Founder of the Dominican Republic

In 1822 Haitian troops invaded and occupied the Dominican Republic. Originally a colony of Spain and then a French possession, the Dominican Republic suffered from an impending bondage that threatened the very essence of its traditions, language, and cultural heritage.

It was during this period of Haitian oppression that Juan Pablo Duarte patiently organized the struggle for Dominican independence.

Born in 1813 to a Spanish father and Dominican mother, Juan Pablo studied and completed his secondary education in Spain from where he returned in 1833. He quickly sensed the harshness of

Haitian control and at once embarked upon the task of achieving absolute freedom from foreign domination.
domination.

In 1838 he founded a secret society, *La Trinitaria,* where entering members swore to ". . . wholly cooperate with a definite break from the Haitian government and to establish a sovereign republic, free from all foreign rule, which would be called the Dominican Republic and which would have on its tri-colored banner a white cross set against red and blue quadrants."*

The treachery of one of its members caused *La Trinitaria* to be dissolved, but Duarte soon replaced it with *La Filantrópica.* Through this second secret society Duarte staged various plays which were designed to stir patriotic sentiments. *La viuda de Padilla* is among the best-known of these dramas.

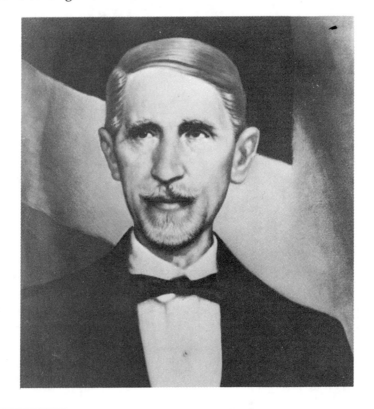

*Marbán, Edilberto. *El Mundo Iberoamericano: Hombres en su Historia.* New York: Regents Publishing Company, Inc., 1974, p. 287.

Motivating his countrymen in every way he could, Duarte was partly responsible for inciting the first independist clash against Haitian troops in 1841. This first attempt to oust the Haitians failed, and Duarte was soon forced to flee from his fatherland. Nevertheless, on February 27, 1844, independence was proclaimed under the leadership of Duarte's followers, Ramón Mella and Francisco Sánchez, and the Dominican flag was raised.

After several months of exile in Curaçao and Venezuela Duarte returned to Santo Domingo where a considerable majority acclaimed him as their president. Duarte did not accept the post, giving a local caudillo, Pedro Santana, the opportunity to take command while pushing him aside.

Nearly twenty years later, sickly and growing old, Duarte again sailed for Santo Domingo. Once more threatened by Haitian invasions, Santana had ceded to Spanish rule. Duarte arrived full of patriotic zest and fighting spirit, but his fellow revolutionaries sent him to Caracas instead on a rather unimportant diplomatic mission.

Duarte died in Caracas on July 15, 1876, a saddened and impoverished man. His remains were returned to the Dominican Republic where they rest, together with those of Mella and Sánchez, at the *Altar de la Patria*.

In 1886, the Dominican Republic newspaper, *El Mensajero*, said: "Juan Pablo Duarte was our first leader, the first to lead us to independence, the first martyr, the finest example."** He was indeed the patriot that paved the way to freedom in the Dominican Republic.

**Ibid., p. 291.

18

CARLOS FINLAY

Dedicated Physician

Long before Columbus discovered America, the ravages of yellow fever were known to the Mayans, the Aztecs, and the Arawak Indians of the Antilles and the jungle regions of South America. After 1492, one expedition of white men after another was wiped out by the dreaded disease. Epidemics of yellow fever were frequent in the New World until as recently as 1900, when the theories and discoveries of a Cuban doctor were accepted and put to use.

Physician and bacteriologist Carlos Finlay was born December 3, 1833, in Camagüey, Cuba. His father, Edward Finlay, was a Scotsman who had studied in both England and France; his mother, born in Trinidad, was of French ancestry. A feeling for international brotherhood and a concern for his fellow man were characteristics of his Scottish father, who while still a medical student, joined one of Simon Bolívar's British contingents and went to fight for the independence of Venezuela.

From an early age, Carlos showed a diversity of talents and interests. As a student in Cuba, he learned English, French, and German. When he decided to follow in his father's footsteps and become a doctor, he first went to study in France and then to the United States. In 1855, at the age of twenty-two, he received his degree from Philadelphia's Medical College. A year later he married a young Irish woman whose family was living in Trinidad. Shortly after, the couple went to live in Cuba, where their three children were born. While the young doctor carried out his most important research, the Finlay children became his first and greatest admirers. In fact, in 1940, twenty-seven years after Dr. Finlay's death, his youngest son published his biography in New York.

For over forty years Carlos Finlay struggled against official disbelief and public apathy. Endless hours of laboratory research often seemed futile.

The thought of thousands of Cubans dying yearly of infectious diseases like yellow fever, tuberculosis, and cholera kept the scientist working long into the night year after year, with only his family's faith and loyalty to sustain him. At first Finlay thought that the saltiness of Cuba's atmosphere had much to do with the spread of yellow fever, but that theory was disproved by the Yellow Fever Commission of 1889.

For the next twenty years few people took Finlay's work seriously. When he first made public the results of experiments indicating that the mosquito was the carrier of yellow fever, even some of his colleagues began calling him the "Mosquito Doctor." But nothing could stop him from developing his theory and presenting his findings at the International Sanitary Conferences of Washington and Havana in 1881. He later identified the genus of mosquito acting as carrier, the *Stegomiyia* or *Aedes Aegypti*. Finlay also explained how yellow fever could be spread by any mosquito that bit an infected person.

American researchers were working on the yellow fever problem at the same time, but they were concentrating on discovering a specific microorganism of the disease. It was Finlay's approach that finally led to the control of yellow fever.

In 1901 a United States Medical Mission headed by Dr. Walter E. Reed, after having failed to control yellow fever, decided to repeat the Finlay experiments. The results were successful and Carlos Finlay's discovery was firmly established and acknowledged by the world's scientific community. In the United States, however, public sentiment has tended to give Walter Reed the credit. For this reason, at the International Gatherings of Medical History in recent years, the following statement is read: "It is confirmed anew that only to Carlos J. Finlay of Cuba, and to him solely, should be ascribed the discovery of the transmitting agent of yellow fever. . . ."

Finlay's long and lonely years of painstaking labor eventually meant life instead of death for millions, since he also made significant contributions to the investigations of other diseases, such as exophthalmic goiter, filaria, trichinosis, cholera, leprosy, and tuberculosis.

In 1902, when Cuba became a republic after half a century of wars of independence, Dr. Finlay was made the new nation's Chief Health Officer—the equivalent of the United States' Surgeon General. He served until 1909, when he returned to his laboratory. The tireless researcher and humanist died at the age of eighty-two, on August 20, 1915. In his honor, the Cuban government created the Finlay Institute of Research in Tropical Medicine, which is in operation to this day. His long and persistent dedication is a source of pride not only to the Cuban people, but to all Hispanics.

19

NICOLÁS GUILLÉN

Black Poet of Latin America

American as well as Latin American intellectuals often say that if the Nobel Prize for literature some day is awarded to a black writer, it will be to Nicolás Guillén.

Actually, Guillén is a mulatto, dark cinnamon-hued, crowned with a mane of white hair. His poetry is one of fierce drum beats, sensuous dark women, struggling city bums, pathetic soldiers, and exploited black slaves all wrapped in an incisive protest against oppression and imperialism. He indicts and ridicules the oppressor while depicting the oppressed with compassion.

Nicolás Guillén was born in the Cuban province of Camagüey, in 1902. His father was a silversmith who became a journalist. In the family library Nicolás read and studied the classics of Spanish literature, while attending the local Catholic school. When he was fifteen, his father was killed by government troops. Guillén had to work as a typesetter to help support his family. Shortly afterwards he began to write and publish poetry.

His first poems followed the Spanish classic style. It was in 1930 that he published his first book of poems based on black, mulatto, and native Cuban themes, *Motivos de son* (Dance Motifs). That was followed by another similar collection, *Sóngoro cosongo* (untranslatable black Cubanese). By that time the young poet was writing exclusively on behalf of the poor, the destitute, and the oppressed of the Caribbean be they black, mulatto, or white. In 1934 he published one of his best-known collections, *West Indies, Ltd.*, which has been translated into every major language. Its purpose is to emphasize American and British colonialism in the islands. In one of the poems Guillén says:

> *Látigo,*
> *sudor y látigo,*
> *tinto en la sangre del amo . . .*

> Lash,
> sweat and the lash,
> stained   with   the   master's
>   blood . . .

Guillén was deeply moved by the Spanish people's struggle against fascism during the Spanish civil war. In 1937 he wrote a poem of epic proportions, *España: un poema en cuatro angustias y una esperanza* (Spain: A Poem in Four Anguishes and One Hope). That year he joined the Communist Party. From that time on his opposition to imperialism and colonialism has produced a poetic fury as seen in his *Cantos para soldados y sones para turistas* (Songs for Soldiers and Dances for Tourists), and in his short, bitter *Canción puertorriqueña* (Puerto Rican Song).

With the advent of the Cuban Revolution, Nicolás Guillén saw his dreams and hopes fulfilled. The following is from one of his most celebrated poems, *Tengo* (I Have):

> *Tengo, vamos a ver,*
> *tengo el gusto de andar por mi país,*
> *dueño de cuanto hay en él,*
> *mirando bien de cerca lo que antes*
> *no tuve ni podía tener.*

Tengo, vamos a ver,
tengo el gusto de ir
yo, campesino, obrero, gente simple,
tengo el gusto de ir
(es un ejemplo)
a un banco y hablar con el adminis-
        trador,
no en inglés,
no en "señor,"
sino decirle compañero
como se dice en español.

I have, let's see:
I have the pleasure of walking my
        country,
the owner of all there is in it,
examining at very close range
        what
I could not and did not have be-
        fore.

I have, let's see:
I have the pleasure of going,
me, peasant, worker, a simple
        man,
I have the pleasure of going
(just an example)
to a bank and speaking with the
        manager
not in English,
not in "Sir,"
but in *compañero,*
as we say in *español.*

Guillén is loved by American poets and greatly respected in intellectual circles in the United States. His collected works, including the *Nicolás Guillén Scrapbook*, are kept in the Schomburg Collection at the New York Public Library. American-Puerto Rican professor, Robert Márquez, of Hampshire College at Amherst has translated an extensive anthology of Guillén's works.

20

FATHER MIGUEL HIDALGO

Architect of Mexico's Independence

During its 400 years of rule, Spain had completely subjugated the native Indian population of Mexico, destroying their culture and allowing millions of people to die of disease and neglect. The natives lived in poverty-stricken villages and worked as peons on large haciendas owned by the Spaniards or by the few local landlords the Spaniards trusted.

This feudal system oppressed not only the Indians, but the creoles and mestizos as well. They wanted to govern their own country and to improve the quality of the lives of the Indians. Although many mestizos were highly educated and owned property, all of them were denied positions in the Church and the colonial government.

Miguel Hidalgo y Costilla was a mestizo born in 1753 on a hacienda in the state of Michoacán. He was a modest man of medium height and a dark complexion that contrasted with his vivid green eyes. Looking at this balding, stoop-shouldered man, one would never believe him capable of leading a revolution that would turn into a war of independence. As a young man, he was an able student. He learned to speak French as well as several native Indian languages. He was interested in world events, especially in North America and in France, where oppressed people were laying the foundations for radical change.

Hidalgo was also a great lover of music. He organized an orchestra among the Indians in his parish and held social gatherings in his home. This was considered to be scandalous behavior for a student of theology, but Hidalgo's behavior was influenced by his secret readings of the Enlightenment thinkers. He was so clever that his classmates called him *el zorro*.

In 1789 he became a priest, knowing that other than the hated colonial government the Church was the only path to advancement in Mexico. But his education and his many abilities failed to earn him an important post because his parents were mestizos. Instead, the Church assigned him to a humble parish in a village called Dolores. At first, the new priest tried to help the Indian villagers by teaching them new methods of farming. But even this made him suspect in the eyes of the colonial authorities. In about 1808, he joined a secret society which was conspiring towards independence. Their plot was betrayed by an informer, and Father Hidalgo was warned to flee. Instead, on September 16, 1810, he rang the church bell in Dolores to gather his parishioners together. He called on them to fight for freedom in the name of their beloved Virgin of Guadalupe.

Led by the rebel priest, thousands of Indians and mestizos marched on Mexico City armed with clubs, axes, knives, and machetes. During their march they liberated many towns as their army grew to 80,000. But at the gates of the capital, they were defeated by the royalist troops.

Hidalgo fled northward but was captured. He was tried by the Tribunal of the Inquisition and sentenced to be shot. On July 30, 1811, he faced his final hours with courage and humor. When asked if he had any last words, he said, "Yes, get me some candy to give to the firing squad." When his last breakfast was brought to him, seeing that the bowl was not filled with milk, he asked, "Because this is the last, does it have to be the least?"

As the firing squad got ready, he placed his hand over his heart to show the soldiers where to shoot. His executioners trembled and could not aim properly. It took many shots to kill him. His head was hung in a cage as a warning to the masses. The colonial government ordered that every picture of him and every book he had written be destroyed.

What the colonial government could not destroy was the need for freedom which the brave priest Hidalgo had awaken in the hearts and minds of the Mexican people. A new generation of rebels took up his banner and kept his struggle raging for years. Mexico became a Federal Republic in 1824, but its national Independence Day is September 16, the day Miguel Hidalgo walked up to the bell tower of his church to ring the bell of liberty for his beloved land.

21

BENITO JUÁREZ

*"Let the people and the government
respect the rights of all."*

Benito Juárez was born in 1806 in the mountain village of Guelatao, near the city of Oaxaca, Mexico. He was a full-blooded Zapotec Indian in a society ruled by whites. His parents, who died by the time Benito was three, were very poor and could not read nor write. He was raised by his grandmother and uncle but they were also poor and illiterate. At the age of eleven, he still could not speak Spanish; he spoke only his native Indian tongue. But his uncle realized that the boy was clever and urged him to get an education.

When he was twelve, Juárez went alone to Oaxaca, where he had the good fortune to meet a bookbinder who was willing to give him a job and teach him the trade. He also sent him to primary school to learn to read and write. When Benito finished primary school, the bookbinder sent him to a seminary, in the hope that he would become a priest.

The young student soon rebelled. He quit the seminary and began to study law. Within a few years he had become a leading political figure in his home state. Unlike most of his fellow politicians, however, he consistently pronounced himself in favor of social reform. He wanted power taken from the Catholic Church, which he saw as an obstruction to progress and justice, just as he wanted to see an end to the tyranny of the powerful landlords. He wanted a bill of rights, as in the United States, guaranteeing the right to think and act freely, and wanted the Indians treated in a more just way.

"The people must work constantly for the destruction of the evil power of the privileged classes," Juárez said. He also said that as long as such classes controlled the government, "society would never be fulfilled."

More than once he was thrown in jail for voicing those ideas. Finally he was exiled to Havana and from there he went to New Orleans. Together with other exiles, he invaded Mexico and succeeded in overthrowing the government.

Although many of his reforms were written into the Constitution of 1857, he was not satisfied and civil war broke out. The people's forces, led by him, were successful and he became president in 1861.

But in that same year Napoleon III of France sent troops to Mexico which drove Juárez out of Mexico City and established an Austrian archduke as emperor. Juárez fought back, but his armies suffered defeat after defeat. By 1867, as a result of United States pressure on the French government, the French troops had returned to Europe. The Mexican people captured and shot the Austrian puppet emperor, Maximilian, and gave the presidency back to Juárez. The country in ruins and its economy in shambles, Juárez's task was not an easy one. He also had to contend with the army generals, backed by the upper classes, who were waiting for a chance to seize power once again.

Juárez possessed the necessary political skills and courage to carry out his reforms, but in 1872, before he could get back into the fray of governing, he suffered a fatal heart attack.

Even the few reforms he was able to institute were swept aside by his successor, Porfirio Díaz, a corrupt general who was interested only in power and personal gain. Yet Juárez is still loved by the

Mexican people who think of him as their greatest president. Among the many monuments and statues Mexico erected as a tribute to him is an impressive bronze figure that stands on a hillside in the city of Oaxaca. Juárez is holding a book on which only one word is carved: *REFORMA*.

The great French author, Victor Hugo, once said that the Americas have produced two great men. One was Abraham Lincoln. The other was Benito Juárez.

22

JOSÉ LIMÓN

Master of the Modern Dance

José Limón, the man who became one of the most outstanding modern dance artists of our time, once thought that male dancers were somehow effeminate.

As a boy in Mexico, Limón enjoyed watching the many kinds of folk dances of his country. When his family went to the United States, he became interested in ballet. Years later he remembered thinking "that it was something for women to do. It never occurred to me as something a man would be caught dead doing."

He changed his mind after seeing a performance by a well-known German male dancer. "What I saw simply changed my life. I saw the dance as a vision of ineffable power." He thought it was something a *man* could take part in with pride.

José Arcadio Limón was born in Culiacán, a town in western Mexico, in 1908. When he was seven, his family moved to the United States; he grew up in Los Angeles. Both of his parents helped develop his sensitivity to the arts, especially music.

In 1928, the young Mexican-American went to New York to study painting. His teachers, however, considered his tastes in art too old-fashioned. Troubled and disillusioned, realizing that it would be impossible for him to conform, Limón left art school and drifted for a time not knowing what to do with his life.

It was at this point that he saw the dance performance that changed his destiny. He immediately devoted himself to the study of modern dance. He had two goals: to become a great dancer and a great choreographer. During the 1930s, he went into choreographing and dancing in Broadway musicals but later, finding it to be too commercial, abandoned this form. "Modern dance is not a popular art," he explained, "It is not for us to advertise automobiles, rugs, vacuum cleaners or hair dyes. . . . You cannot mix the serious form of the modern dance and the commercial form."

Limón first gained national renown in 1943, when he gave six outstanding performances in New York. *The New York Times* described Limón as "one of the most important artists in the modern dance, fulfilling the promise of his early career."

As his fame grew, Limón performed every year in New York City and went on world tours. Dances that he had choreographed, such as *La Malinche* and *The Moor's Pavane*, won universal acclaim. They often had a social theme, lashing out at the horrors of war, poverty, and racial injustice.

"His dance is that of a strong and mature man in command of all his powers," said one critic, "and it gives a completely new meaning and range to male dancing."

During the last two decades of his life, Limón taught dance at various colleges and also made goodwill tours to Latin America, Europe, and the Far East for the United States government. Two presidents, John F. Kennedy and Lyndon B. Johnson, honored him with invitations to the White House. He died in 1973, after a career that gave new dimensions to modern dance.

ET
VRBI
ET
ORBI

NON ALVMNO SED PARENTI, D. F^ro AQVILARIVS. D.   F. LOPIO FELICI DE VEGA CARPIO MVSARVM

Nata fuit Lopio Musarum Sacra Poesis
illa perire potest, iste perire nequit:

104

23

FÉLIX LOPE DE VEGA

Father of the Spanish Theatre

According to Federico de Montalbán (contemporary biographer of the playwright), Lope de Vega wrote 1,800 comedies or theatrical pieces, 400 morality plays, and thousands of poems, interludes, and light compositions.

Lope de Vega is considered the creator of the Spanish National Theatre. In his book, *El arte nuevo de hacer comedias*, published in 1609, he defined the norms for a new type of theatrical work, *the new comedy*, among whose characteristics we find the division of the work into three acts, placing the emphasis on the last half of the third act. He also introduced the use of diverse metrical forms in the same work.

Lope de Vega was regarded as the outstanding figure of his time in Spanish letters. So great was his fame that to praise a work of literature, people often said, "It's by Lope!"

Félix Lope de Vega y Carpio was born in Madrid in 1562. His father, Félix de Vega, was a ladies' man, poet, and gold embroiderer. His mother, Francisca Hernández, who had four other children, came to Madrid in search of her wandering husband.

Lope underwent his primary schooling at the cloisters of the Order of the Teatinos in Madrid. At the age of twelve he ran away to the city of Segovia with a friend. He later entered the service of the bishop of Ávila, Gerónimo Manrique, who encouraged him to begin his studies at the University of Alcalá.

From a very early age, Félix Lope de Vega exerted a magnetic influence on women. He was a tall, dark man of considerable charm enhanced by lively eyes and smooth speech. He was known to be bold and ardent.

As a result of his love affairs, he was forced to live in exile in Valencia for some years. Later, he enlisted in the "invincible" Armada and was secretary to the Duke of Alba.

In 1596 Lope was tried in Madrid on a charge of concubinage. Upon his release from prison he entered the service of the Duke of Malpica. In 1598 he served as secretary to the Duke of Lemos, who was known for his generosity to artists. After living in Toledo and Seville, in 1610 Lope moved into a house he had bought on the Calle de los Francos in Madrid, not far from the residence of Miguel de Cervantes Saavedra, then his rival in fame.

Lope's genius led him to understand, better than any dramatist of his day, the nature of the Spanish people, particularly the common folk. His works reflect his stormy life, which was troubled by amorous passions, and a sometimes violent temperament. But he always felt a deep love for his family.

Between 1605 and 1635, Lope enjoyed ecclesiastical privileges and intellectual distinction. He was a member of the two most distinguished academies of Spain and was made head chaplain of the Order of San Francisco and San Pedro de los Naturales where he received the honorary title of Familiar of the Order of the Holy Office of the Inquisition.

In his worldly life, Lope loved and was loved with passion. He married twice, first in 1588 to Isabel de Urbina y Alderet (the "Belisa" of his verses), a shy young beauty whom he had carried off. She gave him a son and a daughter. After her death, Lope had a number of love affairs, some of only passing interest and others which left children for whom he always took responsibility.

In 1598 he married Juana Guardo, daughter of a wealthy meat and fish supplier. She was a stout and earthy woman, a good housekeeper, and a faithful wife. Five children resulted from their marriage. But Lope, fickle and infatuated, abandoned her for a beautiful actress, Micaela Luján, fiery like him, pleasure-loving, and totally illiterate. He stayed with her for more than ten years during which they had seven children.

Between loves and adventures, Lope never abandoned his greatest passion of all, writing. Someone said that Lope wrote three times as much in his lifetime as any other of his contemporaries. His most representative works are the comedies based on historical events, such as *Fuenteovejuna*, *Peribáñez*, and *El mejor alcalde, el Rey*. He wrote many epic works based on the legends and chronicles of Spain, among them *El último godo* and *Los siete infantes de Lara*. But his most frequently played works are *La dama boba*, *El caballero de Olmedo*, *Gatomaquia*, and *Los pastores de Belén*.

After having been ordained a priest in 1616, Lope fell wildly in love with a comedienne, Marta Nevares de Santoyo (the "Amariles" of his verses), a sweet, refined, and sensitive woman who was married and thirty years younger than the aging author. She had a daughter by Lope and later left him for her former husband.

Lope became seriously ill and performed an act of contrition on his deathbed. His repentance was belated, but sincere.

This world-renowned man, who in his time enjoyed a mythical fame, died August 27, 1635, at his home in Madrid. He was given a magnificent funeral at which both devoted friends and implacable enemies mourned him.

24

JOSÉ MARTÍ

Father of Cuban Independence

A Latin American historian, Jorge Mañach, once wrote: "If one were to choose a single man to represent the spirit of Spanish America, that man would have to be José Martí."

The inspiring story of Cuba's national hero is so rich in deeds and action that the list of his accomplishments would fill several pages of this book. And yet, Martí lived only forty-two years. In that short time he became one of the greatest poets of Latin America, author of dozens of volumes of poetry and prose, founder and editor of four magazines, professor of languages and literature, consul of several Latin American nations in Paris and New York, journalist and art critic for the prestigious American newspaper, *The New York Sun*, leader of his country's fight for independence, and a selfless revolutionary who struggled from childhood to the day he died fighting for the rights and needs of the poor and the enslaved. This genius of a man was human enough to leave us the simple, humble words that today are sung all over the world to the tune of *La Guantanamera*:

> *Yo soy un hombre sincero*
> *De donde crece la palma,*
> *Y antes de morirme quiero*
> *Dejar mis versos del alma.*

> I am a man of good faith
> From the land of the palm tree,
> Before I die 'tis my wish
> To leave my soul in my verses.

José Julián Martí was born in Havana on January 28, 1853. His father, Mariano Martí, served the Spanish Crown as a sergeant in the colonial army stationed in Cuba. Mariano married a young Cuban woman, Leonor Pérez, and the couple settled in a modest house near Havana's waterfront. It was there that José, their first child, was born. From his early days at the local school, it became obvious that the boy was an unusually quick learner. His mother managed to get him into a good private school by the time he was ten. It wasn't easy on a sergeant's salary, but José stayed and graduated, the youngest—and the poorest—student in his class. He also worked part-time as an errand boy and grocery store clerk.

When José entered high school at the age of fifteen, he joined a clandestine club of young revolutionaries and founded *La Patria libre,* an underground weekly. His long patriotic epic poem, *Abdala,* was first published in its pages. But the Spanish government that ruled the island considered any sort of protest to be an act of sedition. José and his friends were arrested. When he was brought to court, Martí made a speech calling for the overthrow of the colonial government. The court responded harshly. Although he was only seventeen, he was sentenced to six years of hard labor. For six months he worked in a quarry on a chain gang with prisoners of all ages, common criminals and political prisoners alike. Slight and slender as he was, his spirit was never broken. "I have suffered much," he wrote to a friend, "but my belief in Cuban liberty enables me to bear it." After a few months, when his chains were removed, he asked the guards if he could keep a few links. He carried them with him from then on to remind himself of the plight of his land.

A friend of the Martí family managed to get José released from prison. However, he was immediately deported to Spain. He studied in the universities of Madrid and Zaragoza, obtained a Bachelor's degree in Philosophy and Letters, and a doctorate in law while supporting himself by writing and teaching. He was twenty-one then. During a brief stay in Paris he met Victor Hugo, the great French writer. But the young firebrand was eager to get as close as he could to Cuba. He went to Mexico first and then to Guatemala. He was becoming famous there for the fecundity and incisiveness of his writings.

Martí married at the age of twenty-four. His bride was an attractive and fashionable Cuban woman he had met in Mexico. He went to Guatemala with her to teach at the Central Normal School. He was professor of English and French literature and history. Although he had been trained to be a lawyer, Martí chose a teaching career because of his deep interest in education. Book learning was not enough, he thought. "Young people have to learn to think for themselves and not believe without inquiry or speak without understanding what a man orders them to think and say." At that time students had to spend hours memorizing and repeating lessons by rote. Martí longed to reform the outmoded system.

When the Ten Years' War ended in 1878, Martí was able to return to Cuba. He found the patriots exhausted and bitterly disappointed. The war had been lost and they had not won freedom from Spain. Martí became the leader of the underground movement. In less than a year, he was arrested and again deported to Spain. This time he left behind his wife and infant son, José.

From Spain he went to Paris, where he wrote, taught, and acted as consul of Uruguay, Argentina, and Paraguay. Finally, believing he could best work for Cuban independence in the United States, he left for New York, "the Iron City," as he called it years later. Here his wife and small son joined him for a while. Some of Martí's most beautiful poems were written for his child and included in a volume entitled *Ismaelillo*. However, his wife Carmen had never felt very close to his revolutionary cause, and she soon returned to Cuba taking the child with her.

Martí made New York his headquarters and most of the time, his home for fourteen years. He learned to speak and write English fluently and became a translator for several American publishers. During many of those years he worked at *The New York Sun*, whose editor, Charles Dana, regarded him as a brilliant writer, critic, and journalist. In his efforts to unite the hundreds of Cuban exiles living in the United States, Martí wrote that "if liberty is not obtainable within, we must bring it to Cuba from without."

Friends and strangers came to his office in downtown Manhattan seeking help, employment, and inspiration. "A brief conversation with him," said a Venezuelan writer, "teaches me more than a year of reading." Martí especially loved children. He took time from his political work to establish and edit—and sometimes write entirely—a children's magazine, *La Edad de Oro*, which is one of his best collections of short works.

In New York, he became consul again and spokesman for several Latin American countries, as well as correspondent for some of their newspapers, among them *La Nación* of Buenos Aires. Here, too, with Calixto García and other Cuban patriots, he planned the next campaign of Cuban liberation. "Wait until the whole island is ready to rise as one man," he cautioned. "To be able to wait is the greatest of virtues."

Martí intensified his efforts to rally Cubans living in exile in the United States and Latin America to their common cause. He traveled a great deal, but always returned to his headquarters in New York and his work at *The Sun*. By 1892 he had organized the Cuban Revolutionary Party and founded its militant organ, the newspaper *Patria*. Men of all walks of life were in the exile movement: students, workers, bankers, clerks, cigar makers, and many others. They suffered serious setbacks, especially when the American authorities discovered and confiscated the cache of arms and supplies they were building.

At last, one stormy night of April 1895, José Martí, leading a group of followers, stole onto Cuban shores and landed at a place called *Playitas*, where they were to join other contingents from the island. It was believed that after some days of consultation with the military men who would lead the patriots in this renewed uprising, Martí would return to the United States to continue sending reinforcements for the war of independence he had helped initiate. But Martí had other plans. He had already written these prophetic words to a friend in Santo Domingo: "A generation of slaves must be followed by a generation of martyrs. Sacrifice must be endured with dignity, grace, and human meaning. For me, the time has come to join the battle."

Against the desperate warnings of his own general, Máximo Gómez, who was leading the patriots in a cavalry defense, the slight figure of the poet, revolver in hand, was seen galloping beyond the front line. He was one of the first to fall in the battle of Dos Ríos, the one that launched Cuba's last war for independence. "El maestro is dead," was the cry that rang that dawn in the Cuban countryside. Indeed, at the age of forty-two, the teacher was dead. The man of good faith from the land of the palm tree had left more than his soul in his verses. He had left the foundation for a nation. Three years later, in 1898, Cuba won the freedom Martí had dreamed of since he was old enough to write his first poem.

25

GABRIELA MISTRAL

"My heart expands to let the Universe enter like an ardent cascade."

The great Chilean novelist and poet, Pedro Prado, a fellow countryman and great admirer of Gabriela Mistral, paints a most accurate and keen portrait of her:

> *Llegará, recogido el cabello, lento el paso,*
> *el andar meciéndose en un dulce y grave ritmo.*
>
> *Tiene la boca rasgada por el dolor, y los*
> *extremos de sus labios caen vencidos como las*
> *alas de un ave cuando el ímpetu de vuelo desmaya.*
>
> *La dulzura de su voz a nadie le es desconocida,*
> *en alguna parte créese haberla escuchado,*
> *pues como a una amiga, al oírle se le sonríe.*
>
> *La reconoceréis por la nobleza que despierta.*

Those who had the privilege of knowing her remember her as a serene yet imposing woman. She was born on April 7, 1889, in Vicuña, Chile and she was named Lucila. Her father, Gerónimo Godoy, an elementary schoolteacher and poet, left home when the child was only three years old. Her mother, Petronila Alcayaga, was a good somewhat rustic woman. She had a daughter from a previous marriage, Emelina, who was a teacher and who, being fond of Lucila, guided her through childhood and adolescence.

Lucila Godoy Alcayaga, impetuous and perceptive, was once sent by her mother to a school where a relative of hers taught. For some reason the teacher judged the young girl to be a very poor student and sent her home with the remark, "Here is your daughter, my friend. Teach her how to sew and cook, for she is otherwise useless." Yet Lucila emphatically refused to do housework, even though she liked it, because she ". . . knew that as soon as they found out that I could do good housework, I would be lost." She never forgot this early incident that compelled her to study on her own and prepare for the life that *she* would choose to live.

In 1905 Lucila worked as a teacher's aide in an elementary school in a small mining town. Her first teaching experience acquainted her with the life of children living in a bad climate without shoes and almost without any clothing.

A year later she again got a job as a teacher's aide, this time in the school at La Cantera. It was here that she met Romelio Ureta, the man who inspired her first book of poetry, *Desolación*. Their intense, tragic love affair ended with his suicide. His reasons have never been learned.

In 1910 Lucila worked as a teacher in the town of Barrancas. She had completed a brilliant examination at the *Escuela Normal Número Uno* in Santiago, and the following year she was promoted to history teacher at the high school level. At the same time, her articles and poems were appearing in newspapers at home and abroad.

By 1913 she was exchanging letters with the poet Rubén Darío, the great innovator of modernism, who at the time was editing a prestigious literary magazine in Paris. Darío received and very willingly published several of the eminently original contributions of the Chilean schoolteacher.

In December 1914, the highly sought after prize of the *Sociedad de Escritores y Artistas de Chile* was awarded to *Gabriela Mistral*—Lucila had by this time adopted this sonorous pseudonym. A triptych entitled *Sonetos de la muerte* accompanied her acceptance statement, but Gabriela herself did not appear. Some said it was because she did not have an appropriate dress to wear. But those who knew Gabriela personally felt that this would never have prevented her from attending the ceremony. She always dressed simply and paid no mind to the dictates of fashion.

The Minister of Justice and Public Instruction of Chile, Don Pedro Aguirre Cerdá, recommended Gabriela as principal of the *Liceo de Niñas* of Punta Arenas in southern Chile. This tract of land is almost deserted, a cold and inhospitable region near the Strait of Magellan often battered by snowstorms. "She was there for two years, in voluntary exile," in the words of Professor Margot Arce of Puerto Rico, "fleeing those places where she had lived the terrible drama of her love." That wasteland was in keeping with her mood and inspired her to express her anguish in desolate poetry.

In 1920 she was transferred to the *Liceo de Temuco* and later to the *Liceo Número Seis* in Santiago. Her high standing as a poet was already recognized in all of the Spanish-speaking countries. She had also been firmly established as Gabriela Mistral. Few knew her as Lucila Godoy Alcayaga.

The year 1922 was significant in her life and work. *El Instituto de las Españas*, of New York's Columbia University, published *Desolación*. Then she was invited by José Vasconcelos, Mexico's Secretary of Public Education, to collaborate in organizing public libraries. On her way to Vera Cruz, she stopped at Havana, Cuba, where she was received with great admiration and friendship. When she reached Mexico, she was given a luncheon at Chapultepec Park by a number of poets. In addition, she inaugurated a school workshop bearing her name at San Ángel. Children dedicated their songs to her.

Desolación, according to the Spanish literary critic Federico de Onís, marked "the complete affirmation of the lyrical individuality of Gabriela Mistral." There was in her voice "tenderness and hardness, sadness and happiness, bitterness and the pleasant taste of honey." The success of this and other work was to take her around the world, and her personal satisfaction at that time was expressed in her *Recados*.

Mistral joined the diplomatic corps in 1932 as the Chilean consul in Naples. Her presence lent prestige to the Chilean consulates in Madrid and Lisbon. She left for Paris because of the Spanish civil war and became a voluntary guardian angel of Spaniards in exile.

In 1938 the three foremost women poets of Spanish America met in Montevideo, Uruguay: Gabriela Mistral, Juana de Ibarbourou, and Alfonsina Storni. It was a great cultural event in Spanish letters. That same year, Gabriela's book, *Tala,* appeared in Buenos Aires, with Gabriela donating the sales proceeds to the Basque orphans of the Spanish civil war whose misfortune she felt so deeply.

A series of painful events occurred in her life between 1938 and 1954, the most terrible of which was the mysterious death of her nephew Juan Miguel, whom she had reared and loved as her own son.

Gabriela traveled constantly, although her health was beginning to fail. In 1945 she received the Nobel Prize for Literature in Stockholm, Sweden. The event had a dual significance. It was the first time that the Nobel Prize was awarded to a Latin American, and it was the first time that a woman poet had received this honor. The news spread like wildfire, shaking the literary world and bringing tears of joy and pride to the eyes of Gabriela's friends, admirers, and countrymen. It was not only the triumph of the girl who had been told to sew and cook, but a just tribute to the woman and the poet who had strewn "bits of her soul" among the brambles of her difficult road.

In 1953 Gabriela joined the Cuban writers in commemorating the Martí Centennial. In spite of her physical exhaustion and ever-failing health, she enjoyed her stay in Havana. She saw her friends and gave interviews, although she tired easily. Her admiration for the Cuban poet-hero is manifest in her essay entitled *La lengua de Martí.*

Sensing, perhaps, her approaching death, Gabriela returned to Chile in 1954 to her Elqui Valley. She longed once more to see her sun-drenched pines and her sad, beloved Indians. She traveled by boat, making stops at every port, large and small, to receive the homage of her people. Strong emotions drained her, yet they seemed to keep her alive. That same year she published her last book, *Lagar,* in Santiago.

After that memorable trip she settled in Hempstead, New York. Her companion was her very good friend and secretary, Doris Dana, to whom she left most of her possessions and the administration of her literary estate.

On January 10, 1957, the brave woman and great poet died in a New York hospital. According to her wishes, her remains were taken to Chile. In Santiago she was rendered the most heartfelt posthumous honors. She was buried in the small village of Monte Grande, "facing the lofty pines and the sun," just as she wished.

26

RITA MORENO

"Never, never give up."

If you ever saw the movie *West Side Story,* you will remember the role of Anita, played by Rita Moreno. Rita was perfect for this film about teenage gangs in New York in the 1950s, for she understands the street life of the city.

Although born in Humacao, Puerto Rico, Rita grew up in Spanish Harlem. Her real name is Rosa Dolores Alverio. She still remembers how puzzling it was, as a small girl, to suddenly hear English instead of Spanish on all sides.

Her talent revealed itself early. She began her career as a child dancer. At first, she performed for free at charity events. Her first performance for pay was at the age of twelve. She earned ten dollars for dancing at a Bar Mitzvah!

Her family was very poor, and at the age of fifteen she had to begin dancing in a nightclub. However, she soon succeeded in finding better jobs. She worked for a radio station, "dubbed" American films in Spanish, and even won a small part in a Broadway play.

Like many young women who want to be actresses, Rita decided to go to Hollywood. But she soon learned that it is not easy to become a star. For a while, she was only able to obtain minor television roles. Then her luck changed. She landed a role in a film called *Garden of Evil,* and her picture appeared on the cover of *Life* magazine. Afterwards came her roles in *Untamed, Seven Cities of Gold*, and *The King and I.*

Her great triumph, however, was *West Side Story,* for which she won an Oscar. "The part I had was a fabulous one," she recalled. Anita was the only real Latin woman of substance—with real guts and soul—that I had ever played in a film."

Anxious to continue her development as an actress and to try other types of roles, she went to London, where she performed with great success in a musical called *She Loves Me.*

Another triumph was to follow. Back in New York on the Broadway stage, Rita Moreno won a Tony Award for her role as Googie Gómez in the musical comedy, *The Ritz.* She can now be seen in the film version of this successful show.

Winning the Tony meant a lot, she said, for "more than anything else, as a person and as a Puerto Rican woman, I feel that it's important to keep going forward as a Latin performer in America. It represents a great deal to my people every time one of us gets some kind of recognition and an accolade in the English-speaking world, because not many of us have really made it in both the Spanish-speaking and English–speaking worlds. That's what the Tony means to me; one more step forward for all of us."

27

LUIS MUÑOZ MARÍN

"We are at war to destroy poverty."

Poet and statesman José Luis Alberto Muñoz Marín was born in San Juan, Puerto Rico, on February 18, 1898. His father, Luis Muñoz Rivera, was a leader, loved and respected by his people. He taught his son two fundamental principles: persistence and patriotism. His mother, Amalia Marín Castilla, also taught him two principles: righteousness and loyalty. This strong moral background molded the character of Muñoz Marín, the man who would teach his people by his example the importance of two other basic virtues: honesty and sincerity.

At the age of thirteen, young Luis got his first impression of the United States when he went to live in New York City with his mother for a short time. When he returned to Puerto Rico, he attended a private school. He rebelled against the strict discipline, but he managed to complete his elementary education. His parents then decided to send him back to New York so that he could learn English well.

The next year his father was named Resident Commissioner of Puerto Rico in Washington, D. C., and Luis moved to the capital and enrolled in Georgetown High School. He later matriculated at Georgetown University, where he studied literature, learned French and English, and wrote literary essays and poetry. During these years in Washington, he made contact with many important people who would help him later in his life.

Muñoz Marín's father fell ill and had to return to Puerto Rico, where he died six months later in 1916. His son was forced to rely on his own resources, and he found a job as the secretary to the new Resident Commissioner of Puerto Rico, with whom he shared an interest in poetry. In his spare time, Muñoz Marín studied in the Library of Congress and sometimes attended sessions of the House of Representatives and the Senate.

Two years later, he went to New York to study at Columbia University's School of Journalism. He managed to make a living by selling his articles and essays to American magazines and newspapers.

After graduation, Luis Muñoz Marín founded a literary magazine. It was while attending a literary meeting that he met Muna Lee, an outstanding young poet and journalist from Mississippi, who soon became his wife.

In 1931, he returned to Puerto Rico and accepted a modest job at the newspaper that had belonged to his father. He joined the Socialist Party, directed by Santiago Iglesias Pantín, with whom his father had always dissented politically. This alliance lasted only a short time because Iglesias favored statehood, while Muñoz Marín advocated Puerto Rican independence. He then joined the Liberal Party and was elected senator in 1932.

Muñoz Marín denounced in the newspapers the island's political corruption and finally went to Washington to seek action. An American newspaperwoman, Ruby Black, introduced him to Eleanor Roosevelt, who was impressed by what he had to say.

Mrs. Roosevelt introduced the Puerto Rican firebrand to her husband, the president.

When President Franklin D. Roosevelt learned of the irregularities in the government of Puerto Rico, he asked for the resignation of its governor, Robert H. Gore. In addition, Muñoz Marín convinced Roosevelt that instead of helping Puerto Rico with money and food, the United States should support a program of industrialization. When Muñoz Marín returned to the island, he was received like a hero. It was his first step in a constant battle for the economic and moral redemption of Puerto Rico.

In 1934, Roosevelt sent a message to the Puerto Ricans, offering his support in the form of the Administration for the Reconstruction of Puerto Rico. Once again, the people cheered Muñoz Marín, giving him credit for that accomplishment. The U.S. Congress provided forty million dollars to launch the operation. An additional seven million dollars was allotted in 1935. But because of interference in Washington and political disturbances on the island, the program was not successful.

In February 1936, a protest led by a group called the Puerto Rican Nationalists ended with the deaths of the American chief of police of Puerto Rico and the two youths who attacked him. Feelings ran high. Muñoz Marín, who was in Washington at the time, was asked to send a message to the newspapers of Puerto Rico, condemning the official's assassination. He agreed, but only if the American authorities would also send a message condemning the actions of the police in killing the two young nationalists.

His attitude won him enemies among some powerful people in Washington. One of them was the senator from Maryland, Millard Tydings, who introduced a plan in Congress offering the Puerto Ricans the choice between remaining a protectorate of the United States or becoming independent. Independence in that form would have meant breaking all relations with the United States, and this might have led to the economic ruin of Puerto Rico. The Tydings Plan failed, but the reaction to it on the island was one of confusion. Strikes and disorders erupted, the Liberal Party split up, and Muñoz Marín was thrown out, together with his many followers.

Luis Muñoz Marín decided to fight back. He went to the streets without money and with only a handful of friends to campaign for a new and different political party. For the first time, the farmers and workers of Puerto Rico heard the plea, "Don't sell me your vote; lend it to me!" It was the voice of honesty and sincerity, and Muñoz Marín got the support he needed. It resulted in the first great victory of the Popular Democratic Party.

In 1944, under the leadership of the Popular Party, Puerto Rico began an intensive program of industrialization called Operation Bootstrap. Muñoz Marín continued to ask the United States for Puerto Rican self-government. In the elections of 1948, he became the first elected Puerto Rican governor. The people's spirits were raised, and the economic situation improved. Four years later, the Congress conferred a measure of independence upon Puerto Rico, making it a commonwealth.

Muñoz Marín was reelected governor in 1952 and 1956. He would have been elected again in 1960 had he decided to run. Instead, he became president of the Senate. Now retired from this position, he continues to advise his government with the same honesty and integrity that have won him a place in the hearts of all Puerto Ricans, as well as in Puerto Rican history. His friends and admirers still refer to him as *El vate*, the bard.

28

PABLO NERUDA

*"I want my poetry to be a war
against cruelty, against injustice
for the liberation of man."*

In 1919, a budding Chilean poet named Neftalí Ricardo Reyes decided to enter a poetry contest for the first time. He thought twice before mailing his entry because he wanted to change the byline. For a last name he chose that of Jan Neruda, the Czech writer, whose work Neftalí had then been reading. "Pablo" was as simple a Spanish first name as he could think of. At last, he mailed his entry. So it was that at the age of fifteen, Pablo Neruda won his first poetry prize. His last would be the Nobel Prize of 1971.

Pablo Neruda was born in 1904. He grew up in the lush southern part of Chile, where his father worked for the railraod. His fondness for the forests and mountains of the region is evident in his very earliest works, which abound in images of humid jungles and wildlife. The youngster also became preoccupied with the struggles of mankind, which was to be the keynote of his most distinctive work.

By his late teens, Pablo was already a well-known activist in the civic affairs of his country. That, coupled with his emerging celebrity as a poet, led him to an early diplomatic career. He was in his early twenties when his government sent him on a series of consular missions to the Far East and later to Mexico, Buenos Aires, and Madrid.

In 1936, at the start of the Spanish civil war, Pablo joined other literary figures of the world in expressing solidarity with the Spanish people against fascism. It is believed that the Spanish civil war marks the start of Neruda's active role in radical politics. In conflict with his government, he was expelled from the diplomatic corps and exiled from Chile.

From 1936 to his return to Chile in 1945, Neruda lived like a veritable poet errant, traveling all over Europe and the Americas, including several stops in the United States. Enveloped in a cloud of political controversy, he returned to his country to receive Chile's National Prize for Literature and was even elected senator. He never stopped writing, however. He wrote about everything that moved, enraged, intrigued, or amused him.

His work ranges from the most exalted romantic sensuality (*Veinte poemas de amor y una canción desesperada*) to his magnificent epic poem addressed to South America, its suffering people, and their toil, *Canto general*. Much of his poetry is satirical, poking fun at his fellow man's most understandable human failings. The way that corrupt governments exploit and dupe the populace was a favorite target of his pen. But his humor could also be warm and gentle and deal delightfully with the commonplace. Witness these lines from his "Ode to the Cat":

> *Camina solo y sabe lo que quiere . . . .*
> *Oh pequeño*
> *emperador sin orbe,*
> *conquistador sin patria. . . .*
> *Mínimo tigre de salón.*

He walks alone and knows his
      pleasure . . . .
Oh small
emperor without a court,
landless conquistador, . . .
mini-tiger of the living room.

Everything Neruda did, he did intensely. He loved animals and nature and kept the most unlikely pets—a badger and a little vicuña, for instance, both of them tame and masters of the household. Collections of natural art works crowded his shelves and walls— seashells, dried leaves, and flowers. He was a gargantuan eater who took three or four hours to dine between sips of wine and snips of wisdom, social criticism, and poetry. "Is there some more?" he often asked gently, long after everyone else had finished coffee. He was a portly man. In girth, even in face, he resembled film director Alfred Hitchcock (both are known to have been delighted at their reported resemblance). His wife Matilde, small, beautiful, and intelligent, hardly reached his shoulder standing on tiptoe.

Neruda was ousted from the Senate in 1948, again because of his radical politics. He had become active in Chile's Communist Party, speaking at election rallies and raising money to support striking workers. He also had angered many with his trips to Russia, where he was given one of their top literary prizes. By then Neruda was firmly established as one of the greatest poets of Latin America. Even those who disliked his calling for Chile's poor to overthrow the privileged classes thought that he deserved the Nobel Prize. Again Neruda wandered all over the world, but this time, as a known communist, he was denied entry into the United States.

In 1970 Chile elected Salvador Allende on an unprecedented platform that called for a government in which all parties, including the Communist, were represented. While Neruda himself did not serve in that government, he supported his long-time friend, Allende, to the end.

In 1971 Neruda was awarded the Nobel Prize. "Poets believe in miracles," he said when the Prize was announced. "It seems that one has happened this time." The intellectuals of the world felt vindicated. At last Neruda had been paid the tribute that he deserved. Many believed that the prize had been made possible because now he was associated with a legitimately elected government. "This is a victory for all of Chile and its people," Allende said. The entire country rejoiced and celebrated. Allende didn't waste time in showing Chile's gratitude to the poet. Shortly after the Nobel Prize was awarded to him, Neruda became his country's ambassador to France and its chief delegate to UNESCO. Even with his demanding diplomatic duties, Neruda wrote every day, if only for a couple of hours. "He has to write," his wife remarked once during those days. "He cannot live without it. If a day goes by that he doesn't have time to sit at his desk at home, he becomes sad, very depressed."

In less than a year Neruda was ill with cancer. He left Paris and returned to Santiago for an operation. During his recovery from surgery, the Chilean government was overthrown by the army. Allende was killed in the rebellion, and thousands of his supporters were jailed. These events seemed to have broken Neruda's heart. Twelve days after the military coup, he died of a heart attack. Much of his library and his possessions were destroyed in the senseless searches that the police and the military carried out in his city apartment and his summer house of Isla Negra. Eventually, the de facto government apologized to his widow and reiterated their esteem for the great poet. But by then, many of his uncopied, unpublished works had been lost.

Neruda's love for his people, so eloquently expressed in his poetry, was reflected in his life. Everyone who surrounded him was his friend; he would even call a stranger by the familiar Spanish *tú* shortly after they had been introduced. He smiled to all, and all were welcome in his home. The richness and humanity of his poetry was a mirror of himself. "That is one of the secrets of his greatness," a friend once wrote. "His poetry unfolds at the same place as his life, deliberate, fecund, jovial, all-embracing."

29

JOSÉ CLEMENTE OROZCO

He painted the soul of Mexico's poor.

In the early years of this century, many young people in Mexico were interested in reform and revolution. They wished to spread new ideas, hoping to help the peasants rise out of their poverty. But the average Mexican was unable to read or write. How could he be reached?

One way was through art. A school of talented painters who were interested in social reform hit upon a devastating formula: depict the suffering of the poor in giant murals.

One of the greatest of these artists was José Clemente Orozco. He expressed the common outlook when he described his own works as "painted bibles." He thought the masses needed them as much as they needed written bibles. Of course, when he used the word *Bible*, he meant not only *the* Bible, but all ideas that the people would need to improve their lot. He wanted to paint murals because they were large, easily seen, and could be understood by almost everyone.

Orozco was born in 1883 in the state of Jalisco. He decided to become a painter after he lost his left hand as a young man as the result of a chemical explosion. His first major exhibit took place in 1915 in Mexico City. Those paintings reflected the strong social awareness that would forever be inseparable from his art.

In the early 1920s, Mexico's revolutionary government decided to commission outstanding artists to decorate the walls of public buildings with frescoes. A fresco is a painting on moist plaster; the pigments work their way into the plaster as it dries. The government chose Orozco to paint a fresco at the main high school in Mexico City. He was soon painting entire murals that were divided into panels, with many characters and events at once revealing an entire story.

Most of Orozco's paintings depict humble Indians and mestizos, although he himself was of Spanish descent. He expressed the sufferings the poor had endured before, during, and after the Revolution. Orozco hated poverty and war, and he yearned to see an end to them. He also felt life as tragedy and sometimes expressed this feeling directly, through faces torn by pain and grief. At other times he used a more indirect method, in which he resorted to irony and a bitter mockery.

Orozco was not an abstract artist whose work puzzles the untrained eye. If you look at one of his murals, you immediately sense what he is trying to say.

The common people of Mexico love Orozco's murals for their honesty and directness. They especially like his paintings of the *Zapatistas*, the guerrilla troops who followed Emiliano Zapata in Mexico's Revolution, and those of Father Hidalgo. Some upper-class Mexicans, however, do not like Orozco's work because they regard him as too critical of the Church and of Mexico's privileged classes.

Orozco continued to paint murals until his death in 1949. He decorated orphanages, schools, libraries, hospitals, and government office buildings. He also painted murals in the United States, including a few in New York City. When he died, the entire Mexican nation mourned his passing. The Congress declared two official days of mourning and ordered that he be buried in the *Rotunda de los hombres ilustres,* Mexico's Hall of Fame.

Orozco had enemies and critics, but he knew how to reply to them. Once he said, "I live in misery. Each sheet of paper, each canvas, each tube of paint, is for me a sacrifice and an anguish, and it is unfair to subject me to scorn and hostility and to insult me."

This intense, sensitive man put himself and his vision of life into every work. The respect he commands in Mexico and beyond its borders is a tribute to his genius. He is part of Mexico's art trinity: Rivera, Siqueiros, Orozco, the three giants of the mammoth art of mural painting.

30

OCTAVIO PAZ

*"A Latin American is a human being
who has lived in the suburbs of the
West, on the outskirts of history."*

A literary critic once attempted to compare the poems of Octavio Paz with those of Pablo Neruda: "Neruda's poetry is like a
fruit—earthy, rich, sweet. Paz's is like the moon—high, cool,
aloof." Well, perhaps not so aloof, as we shall see.

Octavio Paz, Mexico's greatest living writer, today a professor
at Harvard University, was born in the capital of his country in
1914. His mother's family was Spanish; on his father's side there
was Indian blood. His father was a lawyer, and in Octavio's early
years the family lived comfortably. But his father supported
Emiliano Zapata, leader of the poor in the Mexican Revolution, and
as a result of the upheaval, the Paz family lost its money and position.

Octavio did his college preparation in Catholic schools, which some believe may have led to his becoming an atheist. He did not stay at the National University of Mexico long enough to get a degree. *Luna silvestre,* his first book, was published when he was only nineteen. Even that early work is an ode to the things the young poet considered most important—love, ideals, imagination—for he had already rejected the worship of money and material possessions as the primary goal in life. From the start he saw that man had a lot more to contribute to the world than useless trinkets and excessive luxuries.

Seeking to fulfill his vision of life, Paz went to Spain to work and fight against the fascists in the Spanish civil war. When the fascists won, he returned to the Americas. From 1944 to 1945 he lived in the United States, a country he liked very much. He was short of money, however, and when a friend offered him a position at the Mexican embassy in Paris, he jumped at the chance. For the next sixteen years Paz served his country as a diplomat, mostly in undemanding missions that left him with time to write and gave him the opportunity to travel throughout the world.

Paz's best-known book, *El laberinto de la soledad,* was published in 1950. Although written in prose, it deals with many of the themes he had developed in his poems. In it Paz questions history and asks why the Mexican conscience has turned passive and aloof in its approach to life. The poet concludes that the Mexican has suffered too much from the Spanish conquest, from the grip of the clergy, and from the exploitation of the rich and the landowners.

Poetry, history, and philosophy are indivisible elements in the work of Octavio Paz. His wide range of subjects includes world politics, Eastern religions, and the ancient myths of the Aztecs.

His work soon began to receive the recognition it deserved. By the early 1960s his poems had been translated into many languages, and his name began to be mentioned as a candidate for the Nobel Prize. The Mexican government rewarded him with the post of ambassador to India. It was during his years there that he learned, as he says, "a feeling of brotherhood for plants and animals . . . Indian philosophy also taught me to be silent and listen to my own heart," he adds.

In 1964 he married Marie Tramini, a French woman who lived in India. Of that marriage, he says, "After being born, that is the most important thing that has happened to me."

The "high, cool moon" was not destined to be so aloof, after all. In 1968, at the height of his success as Mexico's ambassador to India, Octavio Paz left the diplomatic corps. His resignation was teletyped a moment after the machine had printed news of the massacre of Tlatelolco, where 500 Mexican students had been shot down and thousands jailed for protesting government repression of university freedoms and the persecution of dissenting students. In fact, press services all over the world were sending both stories simultaneously: "Five hundred students shot by government troops in Mexico's Plaza de Tlatelolco . . . . Mexican ambassador to India resigns in protest . . . ." Octavio Paz was *living* his exalted vision of Life and Man.

As his country's most distinguished literary figure, Octavio Paz supports political reform in Mexico, an end to the one-party system, and freedom of expression for all citizens.

Today, at Harvard, Paz teaches and writes, although he insists that writing is what he likes to do the least. He admits, however, that there have been times when writing brought him his greatest happiness. Among his best works are *Raíz del hombre* and *Libertad bajo palabra*.

31

PABLO PICASSO

"I do not say everything, but I paint everything . . ."

Pablo Picasso, who has been called "the restless rebel of twentieth century art," died in 1972 at the age of ninety-one. With his death, the world lost not only a great painter, but also a symbol of freedom. Picasso will be remembered for having produced a greater number and variety of works of art than most artists in history. His legacy includes paintings, etchings, book illustrations, sculptures, and works of pottery.

His personality and lifestyle were as individual and varied as his work. A moody, arrogant, selfish man, he lived his life exactly the way he wanted, changed things completely when he thought it convenient to do so, and didn't worry about his own contradictions or the opinions of the critics.

This led to some strange twists. He learned to draw and paint from his father, an art teacher in Málaga, Spain, but he later dropped his father's name, Ruiz, and adopted his mother's, Picasso. He entered art school at the age of fifteen, passing with one day's preparation an exam for which students usually studied an entire month. Then he dropped out of the school, saying he would rather learn on his own.

He went to Paris and joined the world of struggling young artists and writers on the Left Bank. Like many of them, he borrowed money without paying it back, had many love affairs, got involved in fights, and drank plenty of wine. Unlike many of them, however, he worked hard at developing his talent.

Picasso went through a number of periods during his lifetime. Some of them followed a common color theme. His Blue Period, for example, resulted from a lack of money: he could only afford blue paint, which was the cheapest on the market. He later favored a new color scheme during what came to be known as his Rose Period. Other periods were marked by subjects. For example, there was a time when he painted mostly circus clowns and acrobats. Another memorable series was that of his bulls and bullfighters.

He also adopted several styles. First, he followed Toulouse-Lautrec and Cézanne. Then he became interested in the primitive art of Africa, which influenced the development of an entirely new school of painting called Cubism. Picasso believed at this time that everything in the world could be seen as cylinders, spheres, cubes, and other geometrical forms. By showing a person's head represented in a manner suggesting geometric form, he felt he was getting down to basics.

During his lifetime, Picasso had seven great loves, two of whom he married. Two of the others bore him children. His views on women were simple. "For me, there are only two kinds of women—goddesses and doormats." His last wife, Jacqueline, fifty years younger then he, was his companion, model, confidante, critic, protector, and diplomat. She spent most of her time at his side.

Picasso was very fond of animals. His studio was a haven for stray dogs and cats. His friend David Duncan, the photographer, called it the happiest house on earth. Once, Picasso even contemplated buying a tiger, but he contented himself with less troublesome pets, like a monkey, a goat, and a family of white mice.

In his later years, Picasso was a member of the French Communist Party, though he could never quite remember what the party line was, and never lived the plain and simple life expected of party members. In fact, this communist built up a fortune of fifty million dollars in paintings, real estate, and investments! He was probably the wealthiest painter of all times.

Yet in some ways, he was very serious about his political beliefs. He supported the communists because they fought hard against Franco, whose fascist regime had won the civil war in Spain and had deprived the Spanish people of their civil rights. Like the cellist Pablo Casals, Picasso vowed never to return to his country while Franco was in power.

It was during the Spanish civil war that Picasso painted his greatest work, the 250-square-foot *Guernica*. This painting is a protest against the bombing of a village by the Nazi German planes that supported Franco's army. It is an outraged cry of anger. The figures seem to dive across the picture in terror, heads held high, their mouths open in silent, frozen screams. There are no planes or bombs in the picture; we only see the handful of victims filled with pain and fear. The work is painted in somber shades of black, white, and gray, suggesting a mood of terror and hopelessness. The bombing of Guernica awoke fury in Picasso. In his painting, he wanted to show man's cruelty to man.

By 1939, when France was occupied by the Nazis, Picasso's *Guernica* was safe at New York's Museum of Modern Art. However, an earlier version of the masterpiece was still in Picasso's studio in Paris. One day, the French underground informed the master to expect a visit from the Nazi commandant in charge of the occupation forces in the French capital. Picasso got ready for him. When the commandant arrived at the studio, the painting was hanging on the largest wall.

"What a terrifying scene," the commandant remarked. "Did you do that, Maestro?"

"No, sir," replied Picasso. "*You* did."

32

FELISA RINCÓN DE GAUTIER

*"Love, not politics, is what
gets things done."*

When Felisa Rincón was growing up in the early 1900s in San Juan, Puerto Rico, nobody talked there about "Women's Lib." Young women were taught to devote their lives to the home. They were expected to obey their fathers and husbands at all times. Most young women complied with these unwritten rules, but Felisa could not be like everyone else.

Perhaps this was because other people always looked to her, even as a child, as a leader. As the eldest of seven children, she helped her mother with the young ones. When her mother died, Felisa was only thirteen years old, yet she took complete charge of the other children. Soon her brothers and sisters were calling her *la madrecita*.

Once, when she was still a young girl, she walked into La Perla, the slum where her family's maid lived. There, for the first time, she saw streets of mud, rickety shacks, rats, and children with bellies swollen from malnutrition. It was so different from her own neighborhood of large stone houses, clean streets, and gardens behind locked gates! She ran home sobbing and never forgot what she had seen. From then on, she dreamed of helping the poor and the underprivileged.

In 1932 Felisa went with her father to vote for the first time and realized that she was the only woman on line. She decided to form a committee to get women to vote. Her campaign was successful, and in the next election many women of San Juan voted for the first time.

A short time later, Felisa went to New York. She had always been interested in designing clothes, and she found a job in a dress shop. But soon she felt homesick. She returned to San Juan and opened her own store called "Felisa's Style Shop." It became very popular and eventually all the rich women of Puerto Rico shopped there.

Felisa the designer soon became Felisa the politician. A new political party had been started to help improve schools, housing, and hospitals for the poor. Felisa joined this party and began working very hard to raise support for the cause. At this time, she met Genaro Gautier, a man who shared her dreams of a better life for the poor. They married and started a life together of political involvement.

The party soon asked Felisa to run for mayor, but neither her father nor her husband would permit it. She obeyed them until a tragedy occurred that changed her mind. A violent storm hit the island in 1945, and the slums were flooded leaving thousands of people homeless and without food. Felisa could only give limited help. She realized that before her action could be more effective, she would have to be elected to office, in spite of what her father and husband thought.

In 1946 Felisa was elected the first woman mayor of San Juan. She immediately set out to make many changes, including bringing lights, paved streets, and running water to the slums.

To the people, she continued to be *la madrecita*. Every Wednesday was open house at City Hall. Felisa sat at her desk and listened to the problems of the poor. She saw to it that each one received the help that he or she needed.

Like all politicians, she had many critics. There were always people who didn't like her or thought she was making too many mistakes. Some contended that she was only using the poor people of San Juan to further her own career. Others said that she was too fond of getting her picture in the papers. They also accused Felisa of collecting honors and titles, such as Latin American Woman of the Year, as eagerly as other women collect hats! Even so, the thousands of people she had helped to get jobs or housing supported her as mayor for *twenty-two* years, until she retired from office in 1968.

33

LOLA RODRÍGUEZ DE TIÓ

A Poetic Voice from the Hills

Lola Rodríguez de Astudillo y Ponce de León was born in San Germán, Puerto Rico, on September 14, 1843. A child of well-to-do, educated parents, Lola was destined to become one of the greatest poets of Puerto Rico.

In the cultured and comfortable atmosphere of her home, Lola grew up as a healthy, happy, bright, and somewhat willful girl. Her father taught her reading and writing, while her mother taught her to sing, play the piano, and perform gracefully in society. When the time came for Lola to begin her formal education, she was sent to the best local school. However, the strict discipline of the school system and its educational limitations were too much for Lola to bear. She rebelled and insisted on continuing her education independently, seeking help only from her parents.

As Lola reached adolescence her beauty, talent, and natural charm made her one of the most attractive girls at social gatherings in her town. But she was not just a nice society young lady. She was a woman gifted with remarkable talents, a strong temperament and willpower, and a sense of humanity.

Lola's personality can be illustrated by the following anecdote. One afternoon, while walking with her sister through the streets of San Germán, she pointed to a handsome and distinguished-looking young man. "You see him?" Lola whispered to her sister. "That man will be my fiancé and eventually my husband." Her sister laughed, but Lola did meet the man and eventually became engaged to him. He was a journalist and poet, already involved in the politics of his island country. His name was Bonocio Tió Segarra.

One afternoon, Bonocio passed by Lola's house and found her sitting on the balcony with her mother and sisters. Proud of her beautiful long hair, Lola impulsively pulled off ribbons and hairpins and let her tresses fall on the balustrade so her fiancé could see her in all her splendor. Her mother was scandalized and quickly brought the girl into the house threatening to have her hair cut off if she continued such disgraceful behavior. But Lola's freedom of action was more important to her than her beautiful long hair. She went to her father's barber and asked him to cut off her tresses. At the request of Lola's father, the barber refused to do it. That didn't deter Lola. And so, in a small colonial town unaccustomed to rebellious, individualistic women, she became the first Puerto Rican woman to have short hair.

Lola married Bonocio while still a very young woman. After a European honeymoon the couple settled at home and established a center for literary and political gatherings. Lola's intelligence and strength of character quickly earned her the right to participate in the discussion of liberal ideas with men. This led to her being the first author of the revolutionary song, La borinqueña, which after some changes became Puerto Rico's national anthem.

Because Lola and her husband spoke up in defense of free speech and against slavery, they were exiled from Puerto Rico. For a time they settled in Venezuela, where Bonocio published an edition of his wife's first book, Mis cantares. The work received the acclaim of the critics, and soon Lola was accepted as an important figure in Latin American literature. The publication of her

154

second book of poems, *Claros y nieblas,* won her an award of merit from the government of Venezuela.

Bonocio and Lola spent part of their exile in Cuba. In 1880 they returned to Puerto Rico. But soon after their arrival, the island was in the grip of a new wave of persecutions, arrests, and torture of political dissenters. After protesting to the Spanish Minister of Justice, Lola was able to secure the release of the jailed Patriots, who called her their "guardian angel."

However, political activities again led to the couple's exile. This time they went to New York, where they joined Cuba's movement for independence. When at last Cuba won her freedom from Spain, Bonocio and Lola, with their daughter, went to live permanently in Havana. One of Lola's most famous poems is *Cuba y Puerto Rico, alas de la misma ave.* She loved both lands dearly and found much in common between them, their people, their struggles and their aspirations. Bonocio died in 1905, but the deeply saddened Lola was strengthened and comforted by their daughter, who already showed many of her mother's best qualities.

In her latter years Lola often traveled to Puerto Rico, where she received the love and admiration of her people. She died in Havana, in 1924. The people of her home town have gathered and exhibited her letters, manuscripts, pictures, and favorite objects as a tribute to her memory. Most important of all, her complete works are preserved in a collection of five books published by the Institute of Puerto Rican Culture.

And so, today we, too, can enjoy the sensitive and moving poems of Lola Rodríguez de Tió, the beautiful rebel who became a deep, serene thinker and who contributed so much to the rich heritage of Puerto Rico.

34

DOMINGO SARMIENTO

The Great Educator

Domingo Sarmiento was a fighter for the underprivileged people of Latin America: the poor, the laborers, the cattle herders, the women, and the children. Until this rugged, colorful educator and statesman entered public life, women in Latin America did not, as a rule, attend school or receive a formal education. Sarmiento felt strongly that in an enlightened society, women as well as men should be educated. In his own Argentina, where even women of rich families were often illiterate, he founded a school for girls. But this was only the beginning of his many undertakings.

This intelligent, determined young man began to extend his belief in universal education as the foundation of democracy by starting a newspaper that became a vehicle for spreading his ideas throughout South America. In Chile, Manuel Montt, Minister of Education and Sarmiento's close friend and supporter, once told him, "Ideas, sir, have no country." Nothing would stop the influence of Sarmiento's progressive ideas. Eventually, those ideas spread throughout Chile, Uruguay, and Paraguay, as well as in his native Argentina.

Sarmiento was born on February 15, 1811, in a humble farming home on the slopes of the Andes. His father was one of San Martín's soldiers, and his mother was a strong, handsome woman who loved her country. They both believed that the education of children was the only path to democracy, and so Domingo was sent to school for nine years. He was not very happy at school, except for the time his class elected him to the school government as "first citizen." That event marked the beginning of his political career. Sarmiento was to be the first citizen of the Republic of Argentina.

Despite his formal schooling, Sarmiento was actually self-educated. "I read every book I could get my hands on," he wrote. At the age of fourteen he worked in a humble country store, selling groceries and measuring yards of cloth. But on a nearby shelf was *The Life of Benjamin Franklin,* a biography that comforted and inspired him to become the pioneer and leader that he wanted to be. Years later he said, "No book has ever done me more good . . . . I felt myself to be a little like Franklin, . . . and why not? I was very poor like him, I studied like him, and following in his footsteps, I might one day come, like him, to make myself a place in Latin American letters and politics."

The freedom of expression that he and his family valued so highly almost resulted in his execution during the emerging dictatorship of Juan Manuel Rosas. Fortunately, he was only imprisoned. In 1831, Sarmiento escaped with his family over the mountains, seeking a home in Chile. Although only twenty years old and very poor, he already had developed strong ideas about education. He believed in questioning and experimenting, but he was fired from his teaching job by the governor, who held more rigid and traditional views. Sarmiento then moved on to the port city of Valparaíso, where he worked in a store and tried to learn English in his spare time. He paid half his salary to a teacher, who got him up at two o'clock every morning to study. After six weeks of constant cramming seven days a week, he could read English easily, although he still had difficulty with his pronunciation.

In 1835 Facundo Quiroga, an Argentine caudillo who ruled a large part of the country, was assassinated, and with the end of his tyranny, Sarmiento was able to return to his home town. There he was given a government position. This enabled him to help his beloved country and his people.

It was then that he helped to organize Argentina's first school for girls. He had an admirer in Manuel Montt, the Chilean statesman and educator, who named Sarmiento to head a fact-finding commission to study the education programs of the United States and some of the countries of Europe. The commission was to make recommendations for setting up similar systems in Latin America, where for centuries only the rich had been able to receive an education. Led by Sarmiento, the commission left Chile in 1845 for Spain, Italy, France, England, and finally the United States. It was in the United States that Sarmiento had an opportunity to meet a man he had admired for many years, the educator Horace Mann. Sarmiento was profoundly impressed by the degree of literacy he found in the United States, where he saw people in all walks of life who could read and write, and hopefully go on to higher degrees of culture and enlightenment.

Burning with excitement after seeing his old dreams in action, Sarmiento returned to Chile and published a famous report entitled, *Concerning the Education of the Masses.* He recommended that schools be made available for everyone who had the will to learn to read and write. The report also proposed a teacher-training program in which female teachers would participate as well. It took years to implement Sarmiento's project, but eventually all the measures that he had recommended became law and practice both in Chile and Argentina. He also became director of primary education in Chile when Manuel Montt was elected president. As educators, both men were the main contributors and sponsors of a magazine called *The School Monitor.*

Serving Chile, however, was not enough for Domingo Sarmiento. He wanted to spread his efforts to his own country. He had a chance to do so after another Argentine strong man, Juan Manuel Rosas, was overthrown. Upon his return home, Sar miento was elected governor of his province. Two years later, when he was appointed minister of Argentina to the United States, he left for Washington with the gnawing suspicion that he had been given the foreign assignment in order to prevent his becoming a candidate for the presidency.

A curious thing happened to Sarmiento during his return trip. When his ship made a stop at Rio de Janeiro, he learned that he had been elected president of Argentina *in absentia!* The dynamic and persevering educator served his country in glory and honor for six years. It was an era of peace, culture, and progress in his country. He succeeded in ending the war with Paraguay, founded the Observatory of the City of Córdoba, established Argentina's military and naval schools, and sponsored many important public works.

In 1874 Sarmiento retired to Asunción, the capital of Paraguay, to enjoy its warmer climate and less strenuous pace and to devote himself entirely to writing. There he created some of his most famous literary works, among them *Civilización y barbarie: Vida de Juan Facundo Quiroga,* a book that reveals an extraordinary literary talent and a fine historical perception.

It was in the then quiet garden city of Asunción that Domingo Sarmiento died suddenly of heart disease in 1888. His body was wrapped in the flags of Argentina, Chile, Paraguay, and Uruguay, the four countries he had loved and served so well in a lifetime of struggle that began in a classroom that he, the Great Latin American Educator, never quite liked.

162

35

PANCHO VILLA

Legendary Figure of the Revolution

Pancho Villa is perhaps the most controversial figure of the Mexican Revolution. Like Zapata, he is an idol of the oppressed; yet outside Mexico, particularly in the United States, he is often portrayed as a reckless bandit.

What was Villa really like? To begin with, he was a man of humble origin. He was born in 1878 in the state of Durango in northern Mexico of a poor peasant family. His real name was Doroteo Arango. He later changed it to Pancho Villa, combining his nickname with the surname of a celebrated outlaw ancestor.

Pancho was a rebellious youth. He cut school, begged, and even went to jail for stealing. When he was seventeen, after his sister was raped by the son of a wealthy landowner, he bought a rusty old rifle, lay in ambush for the culprit, and killed him.

In nineteenth-century Mexico, such a crime was normally punishable by death. This was often done by allowing the prisoner to escape and then shooting him in the act of fleeing, the notorious *ley de fuga*. But Villa was more fortunate. An officer took pity on him and did not carry out the plan of execution.

Villa escaped from jail and took to the hills. He became the leader of a gang of cattle rustlers, but government rangers went after him, and he fled across the border into the United States. He joined the United States Army and became one of Teddy Roosevelt's Rough Riders during the Spanish-American War, at which time he learned some of the military tactics he would later use in Mexico.

Villa had already returned to Mexico when the Revolution broke out in 1910. He quickly organized his army. These troops were half bandits and half revolutionaries, like Villa himself. They robbed the rich and often, though not always, gave to the poor.

As a revolutionary, Villa was a man of action, not of ideas. He had no clear concept of what direction the Revolution should take.

Villa became very popular with the poor of northern Mexico but found himself at odds with the basically middle-class revolutionary leaders in Mexico City. There were many conflicts among the different factions. Once, Villa was captured, taken to Mexico City, and imprisoned. During his six months behind bars he learned to read and write and studied Mexican history. Then he made a daring escape and went to El Paso, Texas.

As the civil war in Mexico intensified, Villa returned. He formed an army called *La división del norte* and won many battles in 1913 and 1914. He defeated his main enemy, General Victoriano Huerta, and in November 1914, he joined forces with Emiliano Zapata, the leader of *La división del sur*. On December 6, the two peasant leaders led 50,000 ragged troops in a victorious parade through the streets of Mexico City.

Villa's troops had used *berrendo* tactics to defeat their enemy. The *berrendo* is a very swift Mexican deer that seems to be everywhere and yet nowhere. As one of Villa's followers recalled, "we learned to ride like hell, to eat when we had food, and to sing when there was none. When we had to move fast and silently, we shifted from horse to horse at a gallop. We thought Pancho knew the roads by smell. Many of our men were killed, but others took their place again and again. But how we loved Pancho Villa."

The civil war continued, as did the tension between rival revolutionary groups. Villa kept winning as long as he stuck to his *berrendo* strategy, but he finally made the mistake of trying to fight according to the rules of conventional warfare. This was something neither he nor his troops were trained for. He lost a major battle and had to retreat to the far north of the country. He crossed into New Mexico in March 1916 and looted the town of Columbus, killing fifteen Americans. He made other raids into the United States and also held up several trains. Finally, President Woodrow Wilson ordered United States troops into Mexico to catch him.

Villa and his men made the forces led by General John J. Pershing look like fools. The "gringos" often walked into well-staged ambushes by Villa. False reports of Villa's capture appeared many times in the American press. Finally the United States Army gave up, and Villa returned to his favorite occupation, fighting the *Federales*. But, as the story goes, President Álvaro Obregón persuaded Villa to retire in exchange for an enormous hacienda.

From then on he lived a life of ease as a wealthy rancher in his home state of Durango with his wife and children. He changed titles from General to Don, and many of his loyal soldiers remained as farmhands and cowboys.

Many feared that Villa would come out of retirement and run for (and win) the presidency in the election of 1924. In 1923, however, his car was ambushed near the town of Parral. Villa and his bodyguards were killed. The assassins were never found.

Physically, Villa was a rugged man, nearly six feet tall, with a mustache, red hair, brown eyes, and a sunburned complexion. He usually dressed in khaki, wore a sombrero, and carried a six-shooter.

An American reporter once wrote: "He is the most natural human being I have ever seen, natural in the sense of being nearest to a wild animal. He says almost nothing. His mouth hangs open. He looks rather gentle, except for his eyes, which are never still; they are full of energy and brutality."

Pancho Villa was a popular hero and a legend in his time. His epitaph was a universal sigh of relief and regret. The subject of songs, stories, poems, and films, this man, who was part hero, part bandit, and part myth, continues to spark the imagination.

36

EMILIANO ZAPATA

"I want to die a slave to principles, not to men."

In 1910 Mexico was shaken by the beginning of a mighty revolution. Ever since the death of Benito Juárez in 1892, the country had been run by a few rich landowners. Many Indians and campesinos had lost their land, and the middle classes in the cities and towns had lost their freedom of expression. Only the rich could receive fair treatment because only the rich could afford to pay the bribes demanded by corrupt government officials.

The revolution stirred millions of people into action, resulting in a long and bloody civil war. Many leaders with many different ideas arose and claimed to be the true leaders of the nation.

Emiliano Zapata was different from most of the others. He refused to accept gifts or offers of personal power. He saw himself as the humble servant of the landless peasants and did not want his people to fight and die just so new masters could replace the old. He believed in a society where the power was held by all the people, not only the wealthy, the officials, and the privileged church.

Zapata was born in 1877 in the state of Morelos in south central Mexico. He was a mestizo who helped his father on the farm and also managed to obtain an elementary school education. When he was eighteen, Emiliano lost his father and became the sole supporter of his mother and three sisters. He raised and sold corn and fruit, which he hauled to the village with his mule team.

Zapata was famous among his neighbors as a skilled horseman. One rich landowner was so impressed with Zapata's knowledge of horses that he sent the young man to Mexico City to look over his fine collection of thoroughbreds. Had the gentleman imagined what Zapata's reaction was going to be, he probably would never have sent the fiery young man on that inspection tour. Zapata walked around the fancy stables and saw the floors and walls covered with expensive tiles and marble. He compared this luxury to the mud and straw huts of the poor people back in his village and became enraged. He decided to return home immediately and fight to improve the lot of his people in the countryside.

It did not take Zapata long to get into trouble with the landowners and officials who ruled his home town, men who had been stealing from the farms of the poor, including his own and his brother's. In 1909 Zapata was elected leader of the villagers who were trying to regain some of the land. When the officials turned a deaf ear to the peasants' claims, he organized his people into an armed band. After the Revolution broke out elsewhere, Zapata's men seized land, killed the landowners and officials, and defended the people against the government troops that had been sent from Mexico City to restore order.

Zapata's fighters became known officially as the Army of the South. Unofficially, they were known as the *Zapatistas*. They were hard to defeat because they used hit-and-run guerrilla tactics and had the support of the people in the countryside.

Zapata tried to set a personal example of conduct for his men because he did not want them to become bandits. For example, when the revolutionary armies occupied Mexico City, his fellow leader, Pancho Villa, posed for pictures in the president's chair.

Emiliano refused to do so. He had no use for presidents, palaces, or personal vanity.

Zapata was also a very powerful public speaker. Many of his statements were memorized by the people and are still remembered. For instance:

"Seek justice, . . . not with your hat in your hands, but with a rifle in your hands."

"Land free for all, land without overseers, and land without masters is the war cry of the Revolution."

"Men of the South, it is better to die on your feet than to live on your knees."

In 1911 Zapata and his followers worked out the famous Plan of Ayala. It called for the government to return the land that had been stolen from the Indians by corrupt pre-revolutionary officials. It also demanded that the poor receive one third of the rich landowners' remaining lands.

For many years the government tried to defeat Zapata, but with the support of the people he always won his battles and encounters with the army. The government finally decided that the only way to defeat him was to lure him into a trap. An officer in the government army, Colonel Guajardo, spread the rumor that he wanted to join Zapata with a force of 800 men, and he asked for a meeting. To prove that his intentions were sincere, the colonel massacred an entire government army unit in cold blood!

On April 10, 1919, Zapata went with a few followers to dine with Guajardo at a farm near Cuautla. The colonel had stationed an honor guard in front. When the soldiers of the guard raised their rifles, Zapata thought it was a ceremonial salute. Instead, they opened fire, killing him and his men. Guajardo was promoted to the rank of general and given a large sum of money for this accomplishment. He was never punished for murdering the government soldiers, innocent victims of his ruse.

Although Zapata was dead, the peasants' fight for justice continued in Mexico. He became a legendary figure to many Mexicans. To this day, some villagers believe that he never died and that he lives in a cave in the mountains, ready to aid his people in their hour of need.

Several famous artists, including Orozco and Diego Rivera, have painted scenes and portraits of Zapata and his men. His picture even appears on Mexican postage stamps. In the hearts and minds of freedom lovers everywhere, Emiliano Zapata is remembered as a rider on a black horse, with a sombrero, spurs, a machete, a six-shooter, a big cartridge belt surrounding his chest, and a blood-red scarf around his neck. This was Emiliano Zapata, an honest man who served the people of Morelos, his native state, and of all Mexico without seeking personal glory or asking anything for himself.

EXERCISES

CIRO ALEGRÍA

A. Choose the word that means the same or most nearly the same as the first word.
1. exploitation—a. curiosity b. education c. help d. abuse
2. exotic—a. foreign b. familiar c. easy d. simple
3. devoid—a. full of b. temporary c. tense d. empty
4. rural—a. suburban b. simple c. difficult d. country
5. exile—a. banishment b. welcome c. home d. country
6. principles—a. officers b. policies c. laws d. books
7. convalescing—a. getting worse b. losing time c. getting healthier d. suffering
8. hazards—a. duties b. amusements c. food d. dangers
9. poverty—a. lack of money b. wealth c. lack of time d. idleness
10. downtrodden—a. privileged b. rich c. simple d. oppressed

B. Choose the phrase that best completes each sentence.
1. Alegría wrote about
   a. the geography of South America
   b. exotic creatures which live in the Andes
   c. the problems of South American Indians
   d. the Andes Mountains
2. During his childhood, Alegría
   a. learned to love the Indians
   b. never saw Indians
   c. studied flute
   d. lived in the city
3. Alegría became interested in politics because
   a. he was an intellectual
   b. he wanted to see justice for the Indians

171

c. he was a writer

d. he was banished to Chile

4. Alegría's second book

    a. was about politics

    b. won a prize

    c. was about Gaspar

    d. was about illness

5. Alegría has lived

    a. in Chile

    b. in New York

    c. in Puerto Rico

    d. all of the above

6. During his last years, Alegría

    a. was a businessman

    b. was a publisher

    c. had almost no money

    d. all of the above

7. All his life Alegría

    a. fought for the rights of the Indians

    b. was sick

    c. lived on his father's hacienda in Peru

    d. described the Indians as exotic creatures

C. Put these events in chronological order.

    a. He was banished to Chile for the first time.

    b. He taught at Columbia University.

    c. He wrote *La serpiente de oro.*

    d. He went to Puerto Rico to teach.

    e. *Los perros hambrientos* won a prize.

    f. Alegría's grandmother told him Indian legends.

1.———2.———3.———4.———5.———6.———

D. Answer the following questions.

1. What were the themes of Alegría's novels?

2. Where was Alegría born?

3. Who read him stories and legends about the Indians?

4. Who was one of Alegría's teachers?

5. Why do many South American intellectuals get involved in politics?

6. When did Alegría first go to jail?

7. Why did he go to Chile?

8. Why wasn't Alegría's first book published in Germany?

9. Why was Alegría poor during his last years?

10. Where did Alegría die?

E. **Discuss the following in detail.**
1. Read the poem spoken by *La Antuca*. Do you like it? Why?
2. Why are her parents the Sun and the Earth?
3. Why does the author finish the story about Alegría with his poem?·

ALICIA ALONSO

A. **Choose the word that means the same or most nearly the same as the first word.**
1. bent on—a. against b. determined c. finished d. considering
2. thrill—a. excite b. bore c. lose d. find ·
3. confinement—a. time of training b. time in school c. time of restriction d. operation
4. yearn—a. destroy b. want very much c. plan d. dislike
5. establish—a. fight b. end c. find d. begin
6. titanic—a. huge b. small c. easy d. long
7. affiliation—a. son b. connection c. husband d. country
8. gesture—a. document b. plan c. action d. attack
9. ovation—a. performance b. speech c. shout d. applause
10. frontier—a. limit b. country c. idea d. school

B. **Choose the phrase that best completes each sentence.**
1. Alicia Alonso was born in
   a. Cuba
   b. New York
   c. Europe
   d. the story does not say
2. Alicia married Fernando
   a. when she was a star
   b. in Cuba
   c. while they were still training for ballet
   d. after they joined the American Ballet Theater
3. Alicia Alonso had to undergo an eye operation
   a. after she was a star
   b. before she was a mother
   c. before she was a star
   d. when she was a child

4. She first starred in *Giselle*
   a. when she was ill
   b. before she was ill
   c. when the regular star was ill
   d. when she won the role after a European tour
5. Alicia was considered
   a. the best ballerina in the U.S.
   b. the best ballerina in the world
   c. the best ballerina in Europe
   d. the richest ballerina
6. The Alonsos moved back to Cuba because
   a. they disliked the American government
   b. the American government threw them out of the country because they were communists
   c. they wanted to establish a Cuban ballet company
   d. they wanted to retire from ballet
7. From 1960 until 1975 Alicia Alonso didn't perform in the U.S. because
   a. the Cuban government wouldn't let her
   b. the American government wouldn't let her
   c. she didn't want to
   d. she was ill

C. **Put these events in chronological order.**
   a. Alicia had an eye operation.
   b. She became a star.
   c. She joined the American Ballet Theater.
   d. She began to study ballet.
   e. She established ballet schools in Cuba.
   f. She married Fernando Alonso.

   1.———2.———3.———4.———5.———6.———

D. **Answer these questions.**
   1. Why was it obvious that Alicia would be a star?
   2. How did she spend her convalescence?
   3. How did she get to be a star?
   4. When did she move back to Cuba?
   5. What did she do in Cuba?
   6. Have the ballet schools she and her husband established been successful?
   7. With whom did she dance *Swan Lake* in New York in 1975?
   8. Was this performance a success?

E. Write the correct form of the word in each column.

Noun	Verb
Example: confinement	_to confine_
_____	thrill
_____	yearn
_____	establish
affiliation	_____
_____	perform
success	_____
operation	_____
rehearsals	_____
_____	discover

MIGUEL ÁNGEL ASTURIAS

A. Choose the definition that means the same or most nearly the same as the first word.

1. sorceress—a. cook b. magician c. weaver d. swimmer
2. heritage—a. ancestry b. books c. present d. future
3. stoic—a. loud b. impassive c. excited d. nervous
4. devotion—a. dedication b. disregard c. dismay d. success
5. repressive—a. free b. liberal c. restraining d. relaxed
6. mimicry—a. outcry b. praise c. imitation d. fear
7. theme—a. plot b. character c. setting d. main idea
8. prevail—a. fight b. triumph c. terminate d. endure
9. obscure—a. obvious b. direct c. known d. hidden
10. prestigious—a. impressive b. unimportant c. worthless d. complete

B. Complete each of the following sentences with the best answer.

1. Asturias spent much of his life abroad in
   a. London
   b. Spain
   c. Australia
   d. Paris

2. Asturias' exile from his native Guatemala was self-imposed. In other words, he
   a. was forced to leave
   b. refused to leave
   c. wanted to leave
   d. was asked to leave
3. Asturias believed that the mother of all life was
   a. the earth
   b. the sun
   c. the moon
   d. Central America
4. The Guatemalan Indian farmers
   a. were poor
   b. had no power
   c. were ancestors of the great Mayan civilization
   d. all of the above
5. Asturias had been compared to an ancient Mayan chief because of
   a. his physical traits
   b. his calm, quiet nature
   c. his stoic bearing
   d. all of the above
6. *Leyendas de Guatemala* is a collection of stories that come from
   a. legends
   b. everyday events
   c. his mother's stories
   d. all of the above
7. A dictatorship is a government ruled by
   a. the people
   b. foreigners
   c. one person or a small clique
   d. the navy
8. In *El señor presidente*, Asturias
   a. discusses political freedom
   b. uses symbols
   c. uses words that sound like tolling bells
   d. all of the above
9. When people are exploited, they are
   a. used for someone else's benefit
   b. helped
   c. satisfied easily
   d. given money
10. When Asturias won the Nobel Prize for Literature, he revealed his
    a. modesty
    b. arrogance

c. cruelty

d. boastful nature

C. Put the following events in chronological order.

a. He won the Nobel Prize for Literature.

b. The Nazi dictatorship in Europe fell.

c. Asturias went to Paris as a student.

d. He became Guatemala's Ambassador to France.

e. Democratic government was restored to Guatemala.

1.————— 2.————— 3.————— 4.————— 5.—————

D. Answer the following questions.

1. Who is considered Guatemala's greatest twentieth-century writer?

2. What was praised in *Leyendas de Guatemala*?

3. On what government was *El señor presidente* based?

4. What final impression does the reader get about freedom from *El señor presidente*?

5. What were Asturias' ideas about man's connection with the earth?

6. What is "onomatopoeia"? How does Asturias make the reader hear and feel the tolling of the church bells? Write a few lines of your own in which you use "onomatopoeia."

7. What form of government did Asturias passionately believe in? Why do you think that he felt this way?

8. How did Asturias feel about his novels?

9. What is the Nobel Prize? What qualities do you think a writer should have in order to win this Prize?

10. How did Asturias feel when he won the Nobel Prize? What does this reaction tell you about his personality?

E. Read the paragraph below. Using the words listed at the top, fill in the blanks.

prestigious   deserved   behalf   request

mentioned   award   modesty

In 1967 Asturias won the Nobel Prize for Literature, the most _____ honor accorded any writer in the world. When asked what the _____ meant to him, he replied, with characteristic _____,

"I never thought that I should be awarded the prize, although my name was _____ year after year. I thought it must have been given to Rómulo Gallegos, who certainly _____ it; I was one of those who signed a _____ to the academy on his _____."

HERMAN BADILLO

A. Choose the word that means the same or most nearly the same as the first word.
1. starving—a. thirsty b. lonely c. hungry d. lazy
2. struggle—a. work hard b. want c. relax d. avoid
3. admit—a. elect b. let in c. refuse d. graduate
4. break—a. misfortune b. trouble c. success d. luck
5. vow—a. promise b. ask c. want d. refuse
6. furor—a. pleasure b. excitement c. song d. battle
7. handle—a. disapprove b. approve c. write d. take care of
8. legislation—a. programs b. laws c. schools d. jails
9. set (his) sights—a. was encouraged b. refused c. considered
                              d. made as his goal
10. reserved—a. not open b. friendly c. easy going d. proud

B. Choose the phrase that best completes each sentence.
1. Badillo was raised by his aunt because
    a. she wanted him
    b. his parents left him with her so they could travel
    c. his family was too poor to keep him
    d. his parents were both dead
2. As a child Badillo would not beg for money because
    a. he did not need it
    b. he was too proud
    c. he was not good at begging
    d. his aunt gave him money
3. In New York City Badillo
    a. was poor
    b. had to work
    c. got a good education
    d. all of the above
4. Badillo has been
    a. a politician
    b. a cook
    c. an accountant
    d. all of the above
5. As of 1973, Badillo had not yet been
    a. a congressman
    b. a mayor
    c. a borough president
    d. all of the above

6. Badillo has not fought
    a. against the war in Vietnam
    b. for discrimination
    c. for the rights of the poor
    d. for methadone maintenance clinics
7. According to Badillo, most Puerto Ricans are shorter than most other Americans because
    a. their parents were short
    b. their diet is poor
    c. they don't get enough exercise
    d. none of the above

C. Put these events in chronological order.
    a. His mother died.
    b. He cleaned floors.
    c. He was appointed to the Agriculture Committee.
    d. He ran for mayor.
    e. He moved to New York.
    f. He was admitted to the Bar.

    1.———2.———3.———4.———5.———6.———

D. Answer these questions.
    1. When and where was Herman Badillo born?
    2. Where has he gone to school?
    3. When did he enter politics?
    4. What political jobs has he held?
    5. Why was Badillo's appointment to the Agriculture Committee a "waste of his talent?"
    6. What has Badillo accomplished in his political career?
    7. Why is he a "one-man integration" ticket?
    8. According to his aide, why does Badillo think he doesn't need anybody?

E. Write a short paragraph on what each of these jobs entail.
    a. congressman
    b. mayor
    c. senator
    d. commissioner of relocation
    e. deputy real estate commissioner

RAMÓN EMETERIO BETANCES

A. Choose the definition that means the same or most nearly the same as the first word.

1. comfort—a. attraction b. distraction c. punishment d. consolation
2. adolescence—a. youth b. old age c. maturity d. infancy
3. advocate—a. scream b. support c. deny d. slander
4. epidemic—a. scar b. operation c. widespread disease d. skin
5. unsanitary—a. unfair b. clean c. unhealthy d. progressive
6. hygienic—a. clean b. unhealthy c. cold d. incomplete
7. dedicated—a. vain b. devoted c. superior d. alone
8. reputation—a. disappearance b. notability c. knowledge d. devotion
9. asylum—a. assistance b. refuge c. belief d. strangeness
10. romantic—a. logical b. cautious c. tired d. idealistic

B. Complete each of the following sentences with the best answer.

1. The story is mainly about
   a. a humanitarian doctor
   b. a Puerto Rican writer and doctor
   c. a Puerto Rican revolutionary doctor
   d. all of the above
2. When Betances returned home from France he fell in love with
   a. the landscape
   b. a French aristocrat
   c. his niece
   d. his teacher
3. Betances married
   a. when his fiancée became twenty-one
   b. when his fiancée reached France
   c. after he settled in Santo Domingo
   d. just before he died
4. In Betances' time, Puerto Rico was governed by
   a. the United States
   b. Chile
   c. Spain
   d. France
5. The author calls Betances "a romantic revolutionary" because
   a. he loved his country so much
   b. he was a humanitarian
   c. he was idealistic and lived by his ideals
   d. all of the above

C. Put the following events in chronological order.

a. Betances' mother died.
b. He was named diplomatic representative in Paris by Cuban and Dominican representatives.
c. He met and fell in love with his cousin, María del Carmen Henri.
d. He studied medicine at the Sorbonne.
e. He fought the cholera epidemic in Puerto Rico.
f. He sought asylum in the United States Consulate.

1.———— 2.———— 3.———— 4.———— 5.———— 6.————

D. Answer the following questions.

1. What country ruled Puerto Rico when Betances was a child?
2. Where did Betances study to be a doctor?
3. What disease caused the great epidemic?
4. How did Betances help his country before he was exiled?
5. Why was he exiled from Puerto Rico?
6. What would it be like to be a slave? Describe your feelings.
7. Have you ever been very sick? Tell how you felt and how you were cured.
8. Do you think that such an epidemic could happen today?
9. Can you think of any modern examples where a person has been exiled for his or her opposition to a government?
10. Do you think that Puerto Rico should be given her independence from the United States? Why or why not?

E. Fill in the blanks with the correct answer.

1. Betances _____ both as a doctor and a writer.
   a. revolutionized b. excelled c. annoyed d. failed
2. He was a _____ doctor.
   a. dedicated b. ignorant c. careless d. patronizing
3. When his fiancée died, he was _____
   a. annoyed b. casual c. heartbroken d. happy
4. He was exiled the second time because the government thought they _____ a plot.
   a. participated in b. discovered c. organized d. destroyed
5. Betances was an _____ before he died.
   a. artist b. outlaw c. invalid d. official

SIMÓN BOLÍVAR

A. Choose the definition that means the *opposite* or most nearly the *opposite* of the first word.

1. embittered—a. broken b. miserable c. unhappy d. joyous
2. unruly—a. obedient b. difficult c. headstrong d. uncontrollable
3. impetuous—a. energetic b. impulsive c. excited d. reserved
4. eccentric—a. unusual b. common c. peculiar d. odd
5. liberal—a. tolerant b. open-minded c. narrow-minded d. progressive
6. nervous—a. excitable b. restless c. agitated d. relaxed
7. arduous—a. easy b. strenuous c. steep d. difficult
8. adversity—a. trouble b. good luck c. problems d. sorrow
9. taciturn—a. calm b. quiet c. aggressive d. stoic
10. pinnacle—a. lowest point b. highest point c. peak d. top

B. Complete each of the following sentences with the best answer.

1. Simón Bolívar was born in 1783 in
   a. Venezuela
   b. Spain
   c. Argentina
   d. Bolivia
2. Bolívar's family was
   a. poor
   b. wealthy
   c. aristocratic
   d. both b. and c.
3. Bolívar enjoyed all of the following activities except
   a. horseback riding
   b. dancing
   c. exercising
   d. drinking
4. Bolívar's remark to the young intellectual shows that the former had
   a. a short temper
   b. a good sense of humor
   c. a love of flattery
   d. a love of formality
5. Although Bolívar was a rebellious youth, he became
   a. a priest
   b. a musician
   c. a businessman
   d. very well-educated

6. Bolívar's ideas about freedom were greatly influenced by
   a. the French Revolution
   b. the Spanish Revolution
   c. The American Revolution
   d. both a. and c.
7. Bolívar is considered a controversial figure. In other words,
   a. everyone loved him
   b. everyone disliked him
   c. opinions about him vary widely
   d. opinions about him are the same
8. When Napoleon invaded Spain, Bolívar
   a. tried to break ties with the Iberian Peninsula
   b. joined forces with Napoleon
   c. ran away
   d. went to jail
9. The turning point of the war came when the Royalists were crushed at the
   a. Battle of San Juan Hill
   b. Battle of Bunker Hill
   c. Battle of Boyacá
   d. Battle of Carabobo
10. Before he died, Bolívar felt
   a. happy
   b. disappointed
   c. broken
   d. both b. and c.

C. Put the following events in chronological order.
   a. Bolívar stood on a hilltop and vowed to liberate his country.
   b. He led his troops over the Andes.
   c. Bolívar read the works of Rousseau.
   d. Bolívar won the Battle of Boyacá.
   e. A League of Hispanic-American States met in Panama.

   1. ————— 2. ————— 3. ————— 4. ————— 5. —————

D. Answer the following questions.
   1. Who is called the father of their independence by five Republics?
   2. Who was the liberal French educator who inspired Bolívar's love of freedom?
   3. What three languages besides Spanish did Bolívar know?
   4. Who were the *llaneros*?
   5. When Bolívar fled to Jamaica, what two countries sent several thousand men to help him?

6. How did Bolívar deal with his failures? Describe an incident in which you had to deal with a failure.
7. How have different biographers viewed Bolívar? Can you describe a controversial person whom you have known?
8. What changed Bolívar's mind about Napoleon? Describe a situation which made you change your mind about a person.
9. In what ways did some people begin to turn against Bolívar? Have any of your friends ever turned against you? How?
10. Why did Bolívar prefer the title of First Citizen rather than King? Which would you prefer and why?

E. **From the words listed below, choose the correct synonym for the words in italics.**

> embittered
> unruly
> impetuous
> eccentric
> adversity
> pinnacle

1. As a child, Simón was *difficult to control*.
2. Simón's tutor was an *odd* man.
3. Simón was an *impulsive* young man.
4. During the revolution, he managed to overcome *many problems*.
5. At the *peak* of his career, Bolívar had not managed to totally unite South America.
6. This valiant leader died broken and *miserable*.

JORGE LUIS BORGES

A. **Choose the definition that means the *opposite* or most nearly the *opposite* of the first word.**
   1. genius—a. inability b. inclination c. talent d. aptitude
   2. restless—a. calm b. anxious c. jumpy d. agitated
   3. elusive—a. puzzling b. evasive c. slippery d. obvious
   4. timid—a. scared b. courageous c. shy d. afraid
   5. private—a. personal b. secluded c. special d. social
   6. imaginary—a. fabulous b. strange c. fantastic d. real
   7. transformed—a. changed b. converted c. altered d. unchanged
   8. confusion—a. disorder b. chaos c. order d. turmoil

9. frail—a. weak b. powerful c. delicate d. fragile
10. courage—a. bravery b. boldness c. defiance d. cowardice

B. Complete each of the following sentences with the best answer.
1. The author's main purpose is to
   a. tell about the life and work of a famous Argentine writer
   b. tell about a world-famous writer
   c. show what makes a writer famous
   d. tell about a famous writer's political beliefs
2. The quote at the beginning of the reading implies Borges is
   a. a genius
   b. an alcoholic
   c. an insensitive man
   d. common
3. Borges' father was a
   a. lawyer
   b. cab driver
   c. teacher
   d. both a. and c.
4. The type of stories Borges wrote could best be described as
   a. realistic or naturalistic
   b. dream-like and fantastic
   c. crazy
   d. political
5. It can be assumed that Borges would be most comfortable in
   a. Nazi Germany
   b. Communist China
   c. the United States
   d. Argentina during Juan Perón's regimes
6. Borges married when he was in his
   a. thirties
   b. forties
   c. fifties
   d. sixties
7. Physically, Borges was
   a. strong
   b. mean-looking
   c. ugly
   d. weak-looking

C. Put the following events in chronological order.
   a. Borges' first poem was published.
   b. He was tutored at home.
   c. He got into trouble with Juan Perón.

d. He married his childhood friend.
e. His father died.
f. He lost his library job.

1. ———— 2. ———— 3. ———— 4. ———— 5. ———— 6. ————

D. **Answer the following questions as simply as possible.**

1. When was Borges born?
2. What does his sister do?
3. How long was his first book?
4. Where was he when his first poem was published?
5. What type of stories did he write?
6. Why was he fired from his library job?
7. After what event did he become a national hero?
8. At what two schools in the United States did he teach?
9. How old was he when he finally married?
10. Why does the author call Borges a "man of great courage"?

E. **Facts and Opinions. A fact is something that can be proved. An opinion is something that a person believes or feels. Write either F for fact or O for opinion before each of the following sentences.**

Sample: —— F —— Borges is a writer.
Sample: —— O —— Borges is a great writer.

1. ———— Borges looks like a madman.
2. ———— Borges writes short stories and essays.
3. ———— The Borges family looked upon England as their second home.
4. ———— Borges' first book wasn't very good.
5. ———— In one essay, Borges called for more freedom in using the Spanish language.
6. ———— Borges was immature because he lived off his family until he was thirty-nine years old.
7. ———— Borges' stories were so strange and fantastic few people could understand them.
8. ———— Borges and Juan Perón did not get along well.
9. ———— The United States was Borges' favorite country.
10. ———— Borges said that the world was "all inside me."

JULIA DE BURGOS

A. Choose the definition that means the same or most nearly the same as the first word.
1. premonition—a. mystery b. prophecy c. fantasy d. comedy
2. desparation—a. hopelessness b. desire c. happiness d. eagerness
3. inveterate—a. weary b. hungry c. habitual d. careless
4. extraction—a. invasion b. origin c. attention d. intention
5. quaint—a. tiny b. typical c. common d. unusual
6. reminiscing—a. remembering b. forgetting c. inventing d. receiving
7. shrivel—a. grow b. expand c. wither d. bloom
8. impoverished—a. temporary b. poor c. wealthy d. privileged
9. vibrant—a. energetic b. bored c. fatigued d. dull
10. torrent—a. warmth b. dryness c. outpouring d. drought

B. Complete each of the following sentences with the best answer.
1. The story is mainly about
   a. the poetry of Julia de Burgos
   b. the life and poetry of Julia de Burgos
   c. Julia de Burgos' despair
   d. Julia de Burgos' adulthood
2. Julia's father loved to
   a. read stories to his children
   b. help Julia with her studies
   c. ride horseback with his three eldest daughters
   d. all of the above
3. At school, Julia was
   a. an excellent student
   b. a lazy student
   c. an indifferent student
   d. a disrespectful student
4. Julia went to live with Doña Rosenda because
   a. her family had financial difficulties
   b. her mother was angry with her
   c. she wanted to finish school
   d. both a. and c.
5. When *Poemas exactos a mi misma* appeared, the most influential literary figures in Puerto Rico gave the book
   a. a new title
   b. a new ending
   c. a warm welcome
   d. a negative review

6. When Julia received the prize for *Canción de la verdad sencilla,* she
   a. ignored her family
   b. gave her family some money
   c. got married
   d. went on a vacation
7. Julia could not marry the man she deeply loved because of
   a. rigid social conventions
   b. rigid governmental laws
   c. her poetry
   d. her illness

C. Put the following events in chronological order.
   a. Julia suffered from a terrible depression and had to be hospitalized.
   b. She was found lying unconscious on a New York City sidewalk.
   c. She fell in love and went to Cuba.
   d. She completed the eighth grade and graduated with honors.
   e. She helped other patients on Welfare Island.
   f. Julia joined the Puerto Rican Nationalist Party.

   1. ——— 2. ——— 3. ——— 4. ——— 5. ——— 6. ———

D. Answer the following questions.
   1. Where was Julia de Burgos born?
   2. Why did Julia go to live with Doña Rosenda?
   3. What political movement did Julia join when she was a college freshman?
   4. What institute awarded Julia the first prize for her *Canción de la verdad sencilla?*
   5. What poem did Julia write when her mother died?
   6. When did Julia first become aware of nature? What are some of the wonders of nature that you have seen?
   7. What were some of the deep sorrows in Julia's young life? Have you ever experienced intense unhappiness? Explain.
   8. What is a "premonition"? In what way is *Poemas para una muerte que puede ser la mía* a premonition of her own tragic end?
   9. Have you had a premonition about something or someone in your life?
   10. What does this statement mean to you: "Beyond my life, my words will carry a message"?

E. **Answer the following in detail.**

When Julia followed the man she loved to Cuba, she lived alone in a modest room or humble apartment. All she asked for was a window looking out to the sea.

  a. What kinds of feelings do you think she was experiencing at this time in her life?
  b. Why do you think that the window facing the sea was so important to her?
  c. What kinds of thoughts and emotions does the sea bring to you?
  d. Discuss the meaning of image, simile, and metaphor.
  e. Create some of your own images, similes, or metaphors that express your feelings about the sea.
  f. Now use your own ideas to write your own poem about the sea.

CANTINFLAS

A. **Choose the definition that means the *opposite* or most nearly the *opposite* of the first word.**
   1. humble—a. short b. proud c. modest d. wet
   2. plight—a. bird b. problem c. ease d. predicament
   3. third-rate—a. inadequate b. deficient c. inferior d. excellent
   4. confused—a. organized b. disordered c. circular d. embarrassed
   5. desperate—a. hopeful b. furious c. sad d. dejected
   6. slender—a. thin b. large c. tense d. narrow
   7. nondescript—a. easily described b. anonymous c. random d. indefinable
   8. profit—a. greatness b. gain c. use d. loss
   9. seldom—a. not often b. often c. rare d. royal
  10. sparkling—a. glistening b. twinkling c. alive d. dark

B. **Complete each of the following sentences with the correct answer.**
   1. Cantinflas is known as the world's greatest
      a. singer
      b. dancer
      c. emcee
      d. clown
   2. His real name is
      a. Charlie Chaplin
      b. Mario Moreno

   c. Mario Cantinflas

   d. Mario Valentina

3. He was never a

   a. doctor

   b. bullfighter

   c. medical student

   d. pool hall attendant

4. He was originally

   a. bold

   b. dishonest

   c. unhappy

   d. poor

5. He married

   a. the manager's daughter

   b. an American woman

   c. a cousin

   d. one of his farmhands

6. He is especially popular with

   a. other clowns

   b. rich people

   c. Mexico City's poor

   d. New Yorkers

7. Cantinflas appeared in

   a. an American movie

   b. two American movies

   c. an American circus

   d. none of the above

C. Put the following events in chronological order.

   a. He joined a wandering tent show.

   b. He got a job as a busboy.

   c. Cantinflas made "Around the World in Eighty Days".

   d. He went to medical school.

   e. He married the manager's daughter.

1. ——— 2. ——— 3. ——— 4. ——— 5. ———

D. Answer the following questions.

   1. What do you like best about the circus?

   2. What things make you laugh?

   3. Have you ever seen any of Cantinflas' movies? Which ones? What were they about?

   4. Have you ever gotten in trouble in school or somewhere else for something you didn't do or that wasn't your fault?

5. Are you shy? Tell about a time when you felt shy.
6. Are you a happy person? Tell why, or why not. How do you think one can tell if a person is happy?

E. Write TRUE or FALSE after each statement.
1. Cantinflas is often compared with the great comedian Charlie Chaplin. _____
2. He came from a rich family. _____
3. Cantinflas' name developed into a new Spanish verb. _____
4. He is a very generous man. _____
5. Cantinflas has appeared in many American movies. _____

ALEJO CARPENTIER

A. Choose the definition that means the same or most nearly the same as the first word.
1. physician—a. nurse b. doctor c. lawyer d. farmer
2. rostrum—a. silencer b. illness c. platform d. need
3. compelled—a. allowed b. forced c. freed d. liberated
4. manifesto—a. story b. whisper c. declaration d. silence
5. prelude—a. end b. introduction c. taste d. platform
6. probe—a. investigate b. spoil c. trust d. close
7. protagonist—a. setting b. main character c. theme d. plot
8. myth—a. legend b. history c. fact d. diary
9. immense—a. small b. miniature c. huge d. tiny
10. task—a. job b. pleasure c. guest d. carriage

B. Complete each of the following sentences with the best answer.
1. Carpentier's parents were not
   a. well-educated
   b. sophisticated
   c. intelligent
   d. uneducated
2. Carpentier became a writer so that he could
   a. express his feelings about the serious unrest in Cuban politics
   b. take an active part in the revolutionary movement
   c. become rich and famous
   d. both a. and b.

3. The fact that Carpentier was sentenced to prison for signing a revolutionary manifesto indicates that
   a. he did not know what would happen
   b. he did not think before he signed it
   c. he was willing to take the risk
   d. there was no freedom of speech in Cuba
4. Robert Desnos got Carpentier a visa that enabled him to
   a. get out of jail
   b. visit his father
   c. stay in Cuba
   d. escape to France
5. In France Carpentier
   a. became friendly with the surrealists
   b. realized that the surrealists had a great influence on Latin American culture
   c. developed his own ideas about magic realism
   d. all of the above
6. *Ecué-Yamba-O* is considered
   a. a very deep, psychological study of man
   b. an important work at that point in literary history
   c. a book of poems
   d. an African history book
7. Carpentier believed that the people in the various geographical areas of Spanish America
   a. have their own spiritual characteristics
   b. have a character that links them to the rest of Spanish America
   c. are all well-educated
   d. both a. and b.
8. In *Los pasos perdidos*, Carpentier
   a. feels that the main character (protagonist) is very much like himself
   b. tells about a traveler who has lost his identity
   c. reveals many psychological insights
   d. all of the above
9. Carpentier believed that in revolutionary times
   a. many innocent people would be killed
   b. people should join with the strongest side
   c. ideas are not important
   d. all of the above
10. Carpentier's life implies that to reach one's goal, a person must be prepared to
   a. be dishonest
   b. lose some of his popularity
   c. murder his rivals
   d. join the army

C. Put the following events in chronological order.

a. He became chief Cuban delegate to UNESCO.
b. Carpentier signed a revolutionary manifesto.
c. He went to Paris and met the intellectuals of Montmartre.
d. Carpentier was sentenced to seven months in prison.
e. He wrote *Los pasos perdidos*.
f. His first novel, *Ecué-Yamba-O*, was a failure.

1. ——— 2. ——— 3. ——— 4. ——— 5. ——— 6. ———

D. Answer the following questions.

1. What was the name of the magazine that Carpentier became the editor of in 1924?
2. Why was Carpentier imprisoned for seven months?
3. Why did Robert Desnos get Carpentier a visa?
4. How did the French treat Carpentier when he arrived?
5. Why is *Tiento y diferencias* such an important book?
6. What kind of person is the "protagonist" in *Los pasos perdidos?*
7. What do you think a person would be like if he became a stranger to himself?
8. Have you ever been through an experience in which you felt that you lost your identity? Describe the incident and your feelings.
9. Do you agree or disagree with Carpentier's statement which begins: "Every revolutionary era has its martyrs. . ."? State your reasons in detail.
10. Have you ever lost some of your friends or popularity while trying to achieve a goal? Do you think that it would be possible to avoid this kind of situation? Explain your feelings about this problem.

E. Use the words listed below and place them into the paragraph.

manifesto
pomp
sentenced
diplomatic
visa

In 1927 Carpentier was ——————— to seven months in prison for signing a revolutionary ————. His friend, the French poet Robert Desnos, who was visiting Havana at the time, quickly got him a ——————— so he could flee to France. In Paris, Alejo Carpentier was received with "the ——————— and solemnity of a ——————— envoy."

PABLO CASALS

A. Choose the definition that means the same or most nearly the same as the first word.
1. sensitivity—a. awareness b. hardness c. difficulty d. caution
2. humanity—a. cruelty b. mankind c. correctness d. hatred
3. makeshift—a. unworkable b. temporary c. intricate d. broken
4. suite—a. instrument b. musical composition c. note d. page
5. musty—a. moldy b. antique c. distant d. clean
6. conductor—a. president b. director c. worker d. musician
7. debut—a. beginning b. debt c. operation d. anger
8. totalitarian—a. free b. useful c. dictatorial d. fair
9. transcend—a. obstruct b. travel c. stop d. surpass
10. marvel—a. name b. state c. argument d. wonder

B. Complete each of the following sentences with the best answer.
1. This story is mainly about
   a. a famous musician
   b. learning to play the cello
   c. the loves of a musician
   d. the life and beliefs of a great cellist
2. Casals' father
   a. wanted him to be a carpenter
   b. took him to Barcelona
   c. taught him to play the cello
   d. took him to his first cello concert
3. When the famous conductor Charles Lamoureux first heard Casals play, Lamoureux
   a. acted
   b. hugged him
   c. asked him to learn to play another instrument
   d. threw away his letter of introduction
4. Casals refused to visit Nazi Germany and Communist Russia because
   a. they weren't free countries
   b. they wouldn't let him in
   c. they were at war with Spain
   d. he was a Republican
5. The great missionary doctor Albert Schweitzer convinced Casals to go back to
   a. Spain
   b. performing
   c. the United States
   d. protesting

6. Besides his wife, Martita, Casals loved
   a. his girlfriend
   b. all beautiful women
   c. war
   d. his cello
7. When playing the cello, Casals believed it was best to
   a. concentrate
   b. think
   c. feel
   d. dream

C. **Put the following events in chronological order.**
   a. Casals played at the U.N.
   b. Casals sang in the church choir.
   c. Casals fled to France.
   d. Casals played for Lamoureux.
   e. Casals married a twenty-one year old woman.
   f. Casals appeared in Central Park at age ninety-six.

   1. ————— 2. ————— 3. ————— 4. ————— 5. ————— 6. —————

D. **Answer the following questions as simply as possible.**
   1. Where was Casals born?
   2. When was he born?
   3. How old was he when he first heard the cello?
   4. Who was his greatest musical inspiration?
   5. Why did Lamoureux hug Casals?
   6. How did Casals show his concern for Spain's poor?
   7. Why did he flee Spain?
   8. Who was Albert Schweitzer?
   9. How much older was Casals than his wife, Martita?
   10. What advice did Casals give a cello student?

E. **Often the meaning of a word can be figured out in context by reading the sentence or paragraph in which the word is found. Fill in the blanks using the letters of the correct words from the vocabulary list.**
   1. Pablo Casals showed much _____ toward the feelings of others.
      a. sensitivity b. sensation c. makeshift d. undemocratic
   2. Casals' first cello was not a real one, it was more of the _____ variety.
      a. makeshift b. inspiration c. undemocratic d. humanity

3. Casals opposed _____ governments because they did not allow their people freedom.
   a. humanity b. totalitarian c. democratic d. sensitivity
4. Casals was such a good cellist that he was a great _____ in the musical world.
   a. concern b. performer c. conductor d. sensation
5. Casals _____ to stay in Spain after Franco took power.
   a. performed b. conducted c. refused d. concerned

MIGUEL DE CERVANTES SAAVEDRA

A. Choose the definition that means the same or most nearly the same as the first word.
1. revere—a. ignore b. admire c. punish d. attack
2. innovative—a. creative b. dull c. old d. bitter
3. itinerant—a. angry b. traveling c. quiet d. well-known
4. voracity—a. fatigue b. storminess c. great appetite d. poverty
5. zealousness—a. passion b. indifference c. laziness d. youth
6. confiscate—a. educate b. lend c. give d. seize
7. guffaw—a. scratch b. animal c. loud laugh d. sigh
8. spurious—a. popular b. trustworthy c. fraudulent d. authentic
9. insolent—a. comforting b. delightful c. pleasant d. insulting
10. rancor—a. joy b. gaiety c. anger d. bliss

B. Complete each of the following sentences with the best answer.
1. In his earliest years Cervantes loved to
   a. spend money
   b. read
   c. study law
   d. study music
2. Cervantes' first known work, an elegy,
   a. mourned the death of a beautiful young princess
   b. praised the Spanish army
   c. announced a new Spanish holiday
   d. described his marriage
3. The Battle of Lepanto took place at the entrance to
   a. the Strait of Gibraltar
   b. the Tigrus River
   c. the Bay of Biscay
   d. the Bay of Corinth

4. During the Battle of Lepanto, Cervantes
   a. became ill and stopped fighting
   b. was not wounded
   c. did not fight at all
   d. fought with great courage
5. The galley *El Sol* was attacked by Turkish corsairs, and Cervantes
   a. escaped
   b. was forced to spend five years in captivity
   c. paid the ransom
   d. was gravely wounded
6. Cervantes was excommunicated because he seized grain supplies that belonged to
   a. the French
   b. the Catholic Brothers of the Trinitarian Order
   c. the Cathedral of Seville and Ecija
   d. Turkish corsairs
7. While working as a petty officer, Cervantes
   a. had serious problems with money
   b. had a very easy life
   c. was offered a transfer to the Indies
   d. loved this exciting job
8. While Cervantes was working on the *Segunda parte de El Quijote,*
   a. he wrote plays for Rodrigo Osorio of Seville
   b. Spain became involved in another war
   c. someone else published a phony edition
   d. he was thrown into jail
9. *Don Quijote*
   a. was Cervantes' last work
   b. was never popular in Spain
   c. was never translated into other languages
   d. has been translated into many languages

C. Put the following events in chronological order.

a. Cervantes fought in the Battle of Lepanto.
b. Cervantes was excommunicated.
c. He searched for papers on the street so that he could have something to read.
d. He married a woman who was eighteen years younger than he was.
e. Cervantes was writing *Don Quijote*.
f. He confiscated grain supplies from the Cathedral of Seville.

1. —————— 2. —————— 3. —————— 4. —————— 5. —————— 6. ——————

D. Answer the following questions.

1. Second to the Bible, what book has been the most widely read book in many languages?
2. According to Cervantes, what was "the greatest event that generations either past or present have witnessed"?
3. Who was taken to Algeria as a slave with Cervantes?
4. *Don Quijote* is a parody of what kind of literature?
5. How did the Spanish feel about *Don Quijote* when it was first published?
6. What have you learned about Cervantes from his war experiences? In other words, what kind of personality did he have?
7. Can you describe a personal experience in which you had to act with courage?
8. How did the incident with Osorio of Seville end for Cervantes?
9. What did Cervantes do when he realized that he did not have long to live? What does this indicate about the kind of man he was?
10. What is the meaning of "irony"? Why is it ironic that no stone marks Cervantes' grave?

E. Choose one of the questions below and answer in detail.

1. *Don Quijote* is called an immortal literary work. Give a dictionary meaning of the word "immortal." What do you think are the qualities of a work of art that make it immortal? What other artistic creation would you consider immortal, and why?
2. *Don Quijote* is the story of a "hero" who is constantly confounded by reality. What similarities can you find between this aspect of the hero's life and the author's own life? Discuss elements of absurdity and farce.
3. What is a "prologue"? Write your own prologue, either in prose or poetic form, to the story of Cervantes' life.
4. Draw a time line noting the major events (triumphs and failures) that punctuate Cervantes' life. Now draw a time line of your own life up to the present, and include your ideas about your own future possibilities.

CARLOS CHÁVEZ

A. Choose the definition that means the same or most nearly the same as the first word.
1. vitality—a. flattery b. ignorance c. energy d. anxiety
2. legacy—a. request b. inheritance c. quality d. conversation
3. folkloric—a. different b. traditional c. new d. unpopular
4. immerse—a. finish b. plunge c. yawn d. invite
5. initiate—a. name b. introduce c. soften d. gesture
6. yearn—a. reject b. need c. long for d. try
7. somber—a. cheerful b. useless c. gloomy d. aging
8. harbinger—a. omen b. bird c. athlete d. rage
9. chivalrous—a. huge b. unkind c. scared d. gallant
10. exotic—a. common b. unusual c. ugly d. serious

B. Complete each of the following sentences with the best answer.
1. Chávez first studied with
   a. Erik Satie and Igor Stravinsky
   b. Manuel Ponce and Pedro Ogazón
   c. Leopold Stokowski
   d. Aaron Copland
2. In his early twenties Chávez went to Europe to immerse himself in
   a. European romantic and classical music
   b. modern, twentieth-century music
   c. electronic music
   d. serious Mexican music
3. When Chávez yearned to rediscover himself as a composer, he traveled to
   a. the Mexican coast
   b. Mexico City
   c. the United States
   d. Mexico's jungles and mountains
4. Chávez was inspired by the machine age to compose
   a. "Horsepower"
   b. *Los cuatro soles*
   c. *Sinfonía antígona*
   d. *La paloma azul*
5. Chávez's compositions are
   a. linear rather than harmonic
   b. characterized by simple rhythm patterns
   c. neoclassical
   d. traditional

6. Chávez wrote the ceremonial music for the Olympic Games of
   a. 1956
   b. 1960
   c. 1964
   d. none of the above
7. Physically, Carlos Chávez is
   a. small and pale
   b. awkward
   c. tall and imposing
   d. the kind of person who would not stand out in a crowd

C. Put the following events in chronological order.
   a. He traveled and studied in Europe.
   b. He established the National Symphony Orchestra of Mexico.
   c. Chávez was born in Mexico City.
   d. "Horsepower" was first performed.
   e. He studied native Indian music, traveling in Mexico.
   f. He wrote music for the Mexico City Olympic Games.

1. ——— 2. ——— 3. ——— 4. ——— 5. ——— 6. ———

D. Answer the following questions.
   1. Did anyone in your family sing to you when you were very young? What did that person sing and how did it make you feel?
   2. What kind of music do you like and why?
   3. Do you like classical music? Why or why not?
   4. Which do you like better, the city or the country, and why? What can you do in the country that you can't do in the city?
   5. What are some of the musical instruments from your country?
   6. Have you ever heard any of Carlos Chávez's music? Explain.
   7. In which kind of clothes do you feel more yourself, formal or informal?
   8. Do you think students would work better if there were soft music in the classroom? Explain.

E. Using an unabridged dictionary, find the meaning of the following words.
   classical
   romantic
   traditional
   modern
   culture
Now take each of the entries and define them in your own words.

CÉSAR CHÁVEZ

A. Choose the definition that means the same or most nearly the same as the first word.
1. downtrodden—a. able b. out of work c. oppressed d. satisfied
2. migrant—a. wealthy person b. greedy person c. person who moves from place to place d. protagonist
3. plight—a. comfort b. event c. predicament d. station
4. evict—a. force out b. push down c. desire d. struggle
5. instability—a. sureness b. uncertainty c. fright d. attitude
6. prejudice—a. fondness b. growth c. intolerance d. old age
7. segregate—a. keep apart b. keep together c. unite d. scare
8. nonviolent—a. excitable b. active c. wild d. peaceful
9. deformity—a. leg b. distortion c. humor d. sameness
10. deprivation—a. lack b. gain c. wealth d. communication

B. Complete each of the following sentences with the best answer.
1. The story is mainly about
   a. a great organizer of men
   b. a man who rose from poverty
   c. a religious man
   d. the farm workers
2. During the Depression, Chávez's parents went bankrupt and were unable to
   a. pay their debts
   b. move to California
   c. become migrant workers
   d. join a union
3. César did not go to high school because
   a. he refused to go
   b. he had too many fights
   c. he joined the army
   d. his parents were too poor
4. As he was growing up, César learned that
   a. violence is necessary
   b. prejudice causes suffering
   c. segregation helps people
   d. money is the most important goal
5. At first, César was unsure whether he should try to organize a union or not because
   a. he was afraid to anger the growers
   b. he had a back problem
   c. others had tried and failed
   d. the churches refused to give their support

6. During the boycott of California grapes, people all over the United States supported Chávez and
   a. refused to buy grapes
   b. continued to buy grapes
   c. refused to picket
   d. began to rob supermarkets
7. Chávez feels that in order to win their struggle, the farm workers must
   a. destroy the union
   b. use violence
   c. use only nonviolent tactics
   d. never use boycotts or strikes

C. Put the following events in chronological order.

   a. Chávez organized the migrant farm worker's union.
   b. Chávez's parents were too poor to send him to high school.
   c. The Teamsters beat up the workers who refused to join them.
   d. Chávez went on a fast for twenty-five days.
   e. New farm machines are putting many men out of work.
   f. Chávez led a 300-mile march to the state capitol in Sacramento.

1. ———— 2. ———— 3. ———— 4. ———— 5. ———— 6. ————

D. Answer the following questions.

   1. When and where was Chávez born?
   2. Why did the Chávez family have to move frequently?
   3. Why did Chávez leave his good job with the antipoverty program?
   4. Why did the bosses hire strikebreakers during the 1965 strike?
   5. How many miles was the march that Chávez led to the state capitol in Sacramento?
   6. What is "prejudice"? Have you ever felt prejudiced against something or someone, or vice versa? Explain your feelings, and tell why you think you had them.
   7. Why do you think that many churches, unions, and college students began to support Chávez and his people?
   8. What do Chávez's statements mean to you? "If you win nonviolently, then you have a double victory. You have not only won your fight, but you remain free."
   9. In the above statements, are Chávez's words spoken only to the poor, or do they have an important message for all men? Explain your answer.
   10. How did Chávez feel about death, and why do you think he felt this way?

E. Organize an informal class debate entitled, "Man and Machines: Good or Evil?"

Allow for individual and group research. Students can support their statements and feelings with historical background, newspaper articles, statistics from companies, and personal experience. Have the students identify their statements as fact or opinion. Ultimately, discuss the problem of whether certain questions have clear-cut answers.

ROBERTO CLEMENTE

A. Choose the word that means the same or most nearly the same as the first word.
1. compassionate—a. busy b. rich c. concerned about others d. religious
2. victims—a. sufferers b. workers c. athletes d. helpers
3. acquire—a. sell b. get c. find d. lose
4. moody—a. happy b. contented c. gloomy d. relaxed
5. hustle—a. be lazy b. ignore c. dream d. work hard
6. twinkle—a. sparkle b. be hard c. cry d. close
7. attack—a. leave alone b. fight c. find d. spend money
8. decline—a. say yes b. say no c. agree d. approve
9. homeless—a. making a home b. without a home c. outside the home d. without money
10. admit—a. keep out b. buy c. insult d. let in

B. Choose the phrase that best completes each of the following sentences.
1. Clemente is famous as
   a. a rich man
   b. a doctor
   c. a baseball player
   d. a foreman
2. He played baseball
   a. first for the Dodgers, then for the Pirates
   b. in Puerto Rico, then for the Pirates
   c. only for the Dodgers
   d. only in Puerto Rico

3. During his first few years with the Pirates, Clemente
   a. played extremely well
   b. was very contented
   c. was in a fire
   d. was unhappy
4. Clemente
   a. was liked by his fellow players
   b. was admired by big league managers
   c. played in the World Series
   d. all of the above
5. Clemente was interested in a "sports city" for young Puerto Ricans because
   a. he wanted to attack the drug problem there
   b. he had finished the World Series
   c. he didn't participate in sports when he was a child
   d. all of the above
6. Other team members
   a. felt Clemente was selfish
   b. felt he inspired them
   c. felt he was too big
   d. both a. and c.
7. Clemente was going to Managua
   a. to play baseball
   b. to see the earthquake
   c. to help the people in Nicaragua
   d. none of the above

C. **Put these events in chronological order.**
   a. Clemente died.
   b. He reached the 3,000 hit mark.
   c. He was elected to baseball's Hall of Fame.
   d. He played pro baseball in Puerto Rico.
   e. He began playing for the Pirates.
   f. He signed with the Dodgers.

   1.———2.———3.———4.———5.———6.———

D. **Answer these questions.**
   1. What did Clemente's father do?
   2. How old was Clemente when he began to play pro baseball?
   3. How much bonus did the Dodgers sign Clemente for?
   4. Why was this amount outstanding?
   5. Why was Clemente "the most complete player in the game?"

6. How did Clemente feel about helping other people?
7. Where did he live off-season?

E. **Place the correct word from the list into the correct sentence.**

compassionate	attack
victims	declined
acquired	homeless
moody	admitted

1. Clemente's plan to go to Managua demonstrates that he was a _____ man.
2. After the earthquake people in Nicaragua were hungry and _____.
3. The _____ of the earthquake lost their homes and some of their family.
4. The Pirates _____ Clemente in a special draft.
5. Clemente was _____ to the Hall of Fame in 1973.
6. When he first played for the Pirates, Clemente was _____.
7. Clemente _____ to be mayor.
8. Clemente wanted to _____ the drug problem before it starts.

RUBÉN DARÍO

A. **Choose the definition that means the same or most nearly the same as the first word.**
1. predestined—a. decided beforehand b. safe c. never written d. created
2. precocious—a. hungry b. cheap c. premature development d. silly
3. innovative—a. modified b. old c. repetitive d. careless
4. honorary—a. false b. in name only c. contrary d. endless
5. impart—a. distort b. reveal c. close d. stifle
6. anguish—a. warmth b. evil c. goodness d. pain
7. virile—a. potent b. aging c. immature d. colorless
8. plagued—a. sorry b. tormented c. industrious d. aided
9. pamper—a. spoil b. raise c. expect d. deliver
10. convalesce—a. spread out b. decide c. discover d. recover

B. Complete each of the following sentences with the best answer.

1. The literary school that began and ended with Rubén Darío is
   a. Romanticism
   b. Classicism
   c. Surrealism
   d. Modernism
2. Darío was born in 1867 in
   a. Nicaragua
   b. Guatemala
   c. Chile
   d. Argentina
3. Darío's "humble household" means that his family was rather
   a. weak
   b. poor
   c. wealthy
   d. happy
4. On his diplomatic missions, Darío
   a. went to school
   b. was unpopular
   c. represented his country
   d. helped plan war tactics
5. Darío's aesthetic manifesto stated his ideas about
   a. artistic beauty
   b. the poetry of words and sounds
   c. Communism
   d. both a. and b.
6. Darío's first book was called
   a. *Azul*
   b. *Peregrinaciones*
   c. *Prosas profanas*
   d. *Cantos de vida y esperanza*
7. Darío became very depressed after
   a. his first book of poetry was a failure
   b. his first wife died
   c. he visited a peasant woman
   d. he left school
8. The central theme of *Prosas profanas* is
   a. the hardships of life
   b. the fall of mankind
   c. the joy of life
   d. the evils of crime
9. Tormented by lack of money, Darío began to drink and was
   a. trapped into marriage
   b. unable to marry the woman whom he loved

c. never able to write again
d. both a. and b.

10. Over Darío's tomb is placed a "horrible marble . . ."
    a. lion
    b. bull
    c. unicorn
    d. horse

C. Put the following events in chronological order.

a. The "poet child" wrote essays and poetry when he was thirteen.
b. He was trapped into a tragic marriage with *la garza morena*.
c. He went to New York and met José Martí, the Cuban poet.
d. Darío was buried in the Cathedral of León.
e. In Paris, he met the Symbolist and Parnassian poets.
f. In 1914, Europe was involved in World War I.

1. ——— 2. ——— 3. ——— 4. ——— 5. ——— 6. ———

D. Answer the following questions.

1. How old was Darío when he was honored by the President of Guatemala?
2. Can you name three writers who had a great influence on Darío's work?
3. Why did Darío begin to suffer horrible nightmares?
4. Why did Darío go to visit the peasant woman Francisca Sánchez?
5. Why didn't Darío give his lectures throughout South America and the Antilles?
6. What do you think it would be like to be praised as a "poet child"? Give the good and bad effects of this situation.
7. You are a poet and everyone loves your work; however, you are very poor. How would you feel?
8. Darío's life was full of disappointments. Can you describe the most disappointing event of your own life?
9. What does this statement mean to you? "Words must paint the color of a sound, the aroma of a star; they must capture the heart of the matter."
10. How do you think Darío felt after he was trapped into marrying Rosario Murillo?

E. Answer one of the following.

1. Find a library book of Darío's poetry. Prepare a discussion of your favorite poem for the class. Discuss his use of images and metaphors.
2. Have you ever "seen the world as a question mark"? What does this expression mean to you?

3. Write a poem or a short story, or draw a picture in which your central theme is *joy*.
4. Use a dictionary of literary terms and define "paradox." There is a paradox in the epitaph written by Pablo Neruda for Darío: "A lion without stars, for he who was the creator of stars." Can you explain this statement?

JUAN PABLO DUARTE

A. **Choose the word that means the opposite or most nearly the opposite of the first word.**
   1. invade—a. fight b. attack c. leave d. welcome
   2. patiently—a. in a hurry b. slowly c. stopped d. learned
   3. embark—a. start b. forget c. stop d. learn
   4. absolute—a. total b. complete c. easy d. partial
   5. dissolved—a. split up b. discovered c. joined d. forgotten
   6. hoist—a. lower b. leave c. find d. raise
   7. seize—a. make b. give c. fight d. take
   8. sickly—a. ill b. old c. rich d. healthy
   9. zest—a. tiredness b. wealth c. energy d. problems
   10. lead—a. go first b. teach c. refuse d. follow

B. **Choose the phrase that best completes each sentence.**
   1. In 1822 the Dominican Republic was invaded by
      a. Spain
      b. France
      c. Haiti
      d. none of the above
   2. Haiti controlled the Dominican Republic for
      a. 22 years
      b. 44 years
      c. 41 years
      d. you cannot tell from the story
   3. Duarte founded a secret society
      a. to fight France
      b. to fight Haitian rule
      c. to design a flag
      d. to help poor people

4. Duarte did not become the first president of the Dominican Republic because
   a. he was too old
   b. Santana was president
   c. he was not in the Dominican Republic
   d. he refused
5. After Santana,
   a. Duarte was president
   b. Haiti controlled the country
   c. Spain controlled the Dominican Republic
   d. Ramón Mella was president
6. When he died, Duarte
   a. was poor
   b. was out of his country
   c. was unhappy
   d. all of the above

C. Put these events in chronological order.
   a. Duarte lived in Spain.
   b. He founded *La Filantrópica*.
   c. Santana ceded the Dominican Republic to Spain.
   d. The Haitians were ousted.
   e. He founded *La Trinitaria*.
   f. He was acclaimed president.

1.———2.———3.———4.———5.———6.———

D. Answer these questions.
   1. When was Duarte born?
   2. Where did he study?
   3. Which country controlled the Dominican Republic before Haiti?
   4. Why was *La Trinitaria* dissolved?
   5. What was the outcome of the first fight against the Haitians?
   6. Who proclaimed independence?
   7. How did Santana gain control?
   8. Where did Duarte die?

E. Discuss these questions.
   1. Why do you think the Haitian rule "threatened the very essence of its [the Dominican Republic's] traditions, language, and cultural heritage"?
   2. How do you think Duarte might have motivated his countrymen to fight for independence?
   3. Why do you think Duarte refused to be president? Do you think this choice was a good one?
   4. Why do you think Duarte died "saddened and impoverished"?

CARLOS FINLAY

A. Choose the definition that means the same or most nearly the same as the first word.
1. ravages—a. mistakes b. confusion c. effects d. devastation
2. expedition—a. group journey b. quickness c. message d. route
3. dreaded—a. welcome b. frightening c. inspiring d. powerful
4. diversity—a. challenge b. variety c. jungle d. refusal
5. apathy—a. indifference b. concern c. slavery d. genius
6. colleague—a. enemy b. associate c. neighbor d. friend
7. microorganism—a. large plant b. large animal c. tiny form of life d. small tree
8. painstaking—a. careless b. fruitless c. careful d. bountiful
9. persistent—a. satisfied b. weak c. relaxed d. persevering
10. inquisitiveness—a. difficulty b. curiosity c. reluctance d. indifference

B. Complete each of the following sentences with the best answer.
1. The best title for this story is
   a. "The Conquest of Malaria"
   b. "Mosquitos and Malaria"
   c. "Finlay and Reed"
   d. "Finlay: Doctor, Scientist, Hero"
2. Carlos Finlay's contribution to the conquest of yellow fever was
   a. the naming of mosquitos
   b. the discovery of the transmitting agent
   c. a theory about the effect of salt on the atmosphere
   d. the invention of mosquito netting
3. Yellow fever was difficult to wipe out because
   a. people didn't know how to kill all of the mosquitos
   b. the cause of the disease was not understood
   c. the disease spread too rapidly
   d. none of the above
4. Carlos Finlay's father fought for the independence of
   a. the United States
   b. Spain
   c. Venezuela
   d. Puerto Rico
5. Finlay spent so many hours in his laboratory because
   a. he had access to the most advanced, modern equipment
   b. research was necessary in order to find out what caused the disease

c. he had contracted the disease and was quarantined there
d. all doctors do research
6. Finlay investigated other diseases because
a. he was dedicated to eliminating disease
b. he liked to keep busy
c. it was a requirement of his job
d. he had been ordered to do so
7. Before Dr. Finlay died, he received recognition for his
a. discovery of the cause of cholera
b. establishment of the Finlay Institute
c. discovery of the transmitting agent of yellow fever
d. discovery of the microscope

C. **Put the following events in chronological order.**
a. Venezuela achieved her independence.
b. Finlay married an Irish woman from Trinidad.
c. Finlay joined Simón Bolívar's army.
d. Finlay attended Jefferson Medical College.
e. He elaborated on his theory at an international conference of medicine.
f. The American Army medical team proved his theory correct.

1. ——— 2. ——— 3. ——— 4. ——— 5. ——— 6. ———

D. **Answer the following questions.**
1. Why was yellow fever so dangerous?
2. Where did Carlos Finlay go to medical school?
3. When did he become a doctor?
4. How much time did he spend on research on yellow fever?
5. What did Dr. Finlay discover?
6. What is a "biography"? Who published a biography of Dr. Finlay? If you wanted to write a biography, about whom would you write it, and why?
7. For over forty years, Dr. Finlay struggled with his experiments, as well as with official disbelief and public apathy. What kind of man do you think he was to be able to do this?
8. How do you think Dr. Finlay felt when his discoveries were finally acknowledged by the world's great scientists?
9. Have you ever struggled very hard with a project (either at school, at work, or at home) and finally had it favorably accepted by other people? Describe your feelings.
10. Why is Dr. Finlay's discovery a source of pride, not only to the Cubans, but also to people everywhere? Do you think that all men and women, no matter what their country of origin, can feel pride in such an accomplishment? Explain your answer.

E. Answer the following questions.

1. If you wanted to find out about Dr. Finlay's scientific work, where in the library would you look?
2. If you were interested in Dr. Finlay's life, where would you look?
3. If you wanted to write a report about Simón Bolívar, where would you look?
4. If you wished to find information about the American Army Medical Corps' work on malaria, where would you look?
5. If you wished to read the play, *Yellowjacket*, where would you look?

NICOLÁS GUILLÉN

A. Choose the word that means the same or most nearly the same as the first word.

1. awarded—a. found b. given c. sold d. lost
2. sensuous—a. voluptuous b. plain c. poor d. pitiful
3. pathetic—a. old b. injured c. happy d. pitiful
4. incisive—a. loud b. sharp c. angry d. weak
5. indict—a. accuse b. excuse c. refuse d. appreciate
6. depict—a. accuse b. help c. judge d. describe
7. exclusively—a. angrily b. happily c. totally d. loudly
8. fury—a. happiness b. loss c. writing d. anger
9. advent—a. coming b. departure c. success d. failure
10. celebrated—a. long b. profitable c. famous d. simple

B. Choose the phrase that best completes each sentence.

1. At the time this article was written, Guillén
   a. had won the Nobel Prize
   b. was a young man
   c. was a typesetter
   d. had not received the Nobel Prize
2. As a child Guillén
   a. did not go to school
   b. was educated
   c. was very poor
   d. was a published poet

212

3. One reason that Guillén learned to hate oppression by governments was that
    a. his family was very poor
    b. he had to work as a child
    c. his father was killed by the government
    d. his father was a silversmith
4. During the Spanish civil war Guillén
    a. fought the fascists
    b. fought in Spain
    c. wrote poetry against the fascists
    d. was not interested in the fight
5. When the Cuban Revolution came, Guillén
    a. was happy
    b. was angry
    c. was indifferent
    d. was jailed
6. The poem *Tengo* is about
    a. owning lots of things
    b. the problems Guillén has now
    c. the new freedom in Cuba
    d. the pleasure of walking in the country
7. In the United States Guillén
    a. is ignored
    b. is admired
    c. is hated
    d. is not published

C. Put these events in chronological order.

    a. Guillén wrote *Tengo*.
    b. He began to work.
    c. He attended a Catholic school.
    d. The Cuban Revolution came.
    e. His father died.
    f. The Spanish civil war occurred.

1.———2.———3.———4.———5.———6.———

D. Answer these questions.

1. Where was Guillén born?
2. How do you know his family was educated?
3. Where do the themes of *Motivos de son* come from?
4. In the poem *España: un poema en cuatro angustias y una esperanza,* what do you think the one hope is?
5. What is the freedom expressed in *Tengo*?

6. Where can you find the works of Guillén in the U.S.?
7. Do you think Guillén is a happy man today? Why or why not?

E. **Fill in each blank with the best word from the list. Use each word only once.**

oppressed   fulfilled
ridicules   pleasure
mane   fascism
old   translated
joined   charm

1. I have the _____ of walking in my country.
2. Guillén is a mulatto crowned with a _____ of white hair.
3. Guillén indicts and _____ the oppressor.
4. He depicts the oppressed with the most human _____.
5. Guillén wrote exclusively on behalf of the poor and _____.
6. "West Indies, Ltd." has been _____ into every major language.
7. In 1937 Guillén _____ the Communist Party.
8. There is nothing _____ about his writing.
9. The Cuban Revolution _____ Guillén's dreams and hopes.
10. The people of Spain fought against _____.

FATHER MIGUEL HIDALGO

A. **Choose the definition that means the same or most nearly the same as the first word.**
1. subjugate—a. overthrow b. yield c. step aside d. conquer
2. neglect—a. hunger b. indifference c. illness d. poverty
3. modest—a. wealthy b. arrogant c. poor d. humble
4. complexion—a. result b. appearance c. change d. beard
5. vivid—a. lively b. downcast c. silent d. generous
6. oppressed—a. lucky b. established c. persecuted d. grotesque
7. radical—a. extreme b. chemical c. strong d. loud
8. scandalous—a. pure b. intuitive c. sick d. shameful

9. tribunal—a. fire b. court c. meal d. interpretation
10. executioners—a. killers b. helpers c. soldiers d. friends

B. Complete each of the following sentences with the best answer.

1. Hidalgo was not
   a. a priest with a sense of humor
   b. afraid of death
   c. a leader in a time of crisis
   d. an able student when he was young
2. The native Mexicans could not make their own laws because
   a. they were ruled by the King of Spain, who lived 5000 miles away
   b. they couldn't read or write
   c. they had no lawyers or judges
   d. they lacked a legal background
3. According to the author, it is hard to believe that Hidalgo
   a. was really a priest
   b. was courageous
   c. would lead a revolution
   d. was truly dedicated to his people
4. His classmates called Hidalgo "el zorro" because he
   a. was clever
   b. was studying theology
   c. loved animals
   d. secretly read the thinkers of the Enlightenment
5. When Hidalgo asked for some candy to give to the firing squad, this showed that
   a. he really wanted to bribe the soldiers
   b. he had gone insane
   c. he believed it was better to give than to receive
   d. he was able to show humor even at his death
6. The people who suffered most under the feudal system were the
   a. peons
   b. haciendas
   c. Spaniards
   d. local landlords
7. An informer is a person who
   a. tells stories
   b. secretly tells on his presumed friends
   c. has a wealth of information
   d. likes to know what is happening

C. Put the following events in chronological order.

a. Hidalgo was born on a hacienda.
b. He became a priest.

c. He rang the church bell in Dolores instead of fleeing.
d. He showed the soldiers where to shoot him.
e. He was assigned to a small parish in Dolores.
f. He led an army of 80,000 to the gates of Mexico City.

1. ———— 2. ———— 3. ———— 4. ———— 5. ———— 6. ————

D. **Answer the following questions as simply as possible.**
1. What are Creoles and Mestizos?
2. How tall was Hidalgo?
3. What did Hidalgo organize among his parish Indians?
4. Why did Hidalgo become a priest?
5. Why was he not given an important church post?
6. Where was he assigned by the Church?
7. How large was Hidalgo's army?
8. How did he face his last hours?
9. When was he executed?
10. Why is September 16 significant in Mexico?

BENITO JUÁREZ

A. **Choose the definition that means the same or most nearly the same as the first word.**
1. illiterate—a. capable b. educated c. uneducated d. foolish
2. urge—a. disappoint b. force c. encourage d. demand
3. seminary—a. school b. class c. chalkboard d. teacher
4. obstruction—a. defense b. guarantee c. contribution d. obstacle
5. exile—a. outcast b. foreigner c. guest d. motive
6. seize—a. throw b. usurp c. accept d. reject
7. fray—a. dispute b. game c. war d. agreement
8. fatal—a. dangerous b. deadly c. serious d. grave
9. institute—a. finish b. organize c. give in d. complicate
10. successor—a. student b. one who follows c. doctor d. revolutionary

B. **Complete each of the following sentences with the best answer.**
1. Benito Juárez's family was
   a. rich
   b. educated

   c. illiterate

   d. none of the above

2. Juárez was not Spanish. He was

   a. Puerto Rican

   b. Dominican

   c. French

   d. a full-blooded Indian

3. His patron, the bookbinder, sent Benito to a seminary because he wanted the boy to eventually become a

   a. teacher

   b. politician

   c. general

   d. priest

4. Juárez wanted to help free his people from

   a. debt

   b. the landlords

   c. ignorance

   d. all of the above

5. In New Orleans, Juárez worked hard

   a. to get a college degree

   b. to pass his bar exams

   c. for the overthrow of the government of Mexico

   d. to find a good job

6. Juárez became the head of the Mexican government after

   a. an election

   b. a civil war

   c. the conquest of France

   d. he was married

7. Juárez's sudden death left Mexico at the mercy of

   a. the army and General Díaz

   b. the Indians

   c. the United States

   d. France

C. Put the following events in chronological order.

   a. Juárez became a politician.

   b. He left the seminary to become a lawyer.

   c. Juárez was sent to school.

   d. He was jailed and exiled and went to New Orleans, where he organized a revolt.

   e. He was caught on a lake in a terrible storm.

   f. He became the president of Mexico.

1. ——— 2. ——— 3. ——— 4. ——— 5. ——— 6. ———

D. Answer the following questions as simply as possible.

1. Why was it hard for Juárez to get an education?
2. Why were the Indians so downtrodden?
3. To what city was Juárez exiled?
4. What kind of political reforms did he suggest?
5. When did Juárez become president of Mexico?
6. Which European nation sent troops to conquer Mexico?
7. Who became "emperor" of Mexico?
8. What happened to him?
9. What happened to Juárez?
10. Where is there a memorial to Benito Juárez?

E. Look up the following names in an encyclopedia. Write a short biography from one of the articles, in your own words.

1. Benito Juárez
2. the Archduke Maximilian of Austria
3. Porifirio Díaz
4. Emperor Napoleon III of France

JOSÉ LIMÓN

A. Choose the word that means the same or most nearly the same as the first word.

1. outstanding—a. terrible b. rich c. excellent d. poor
2. sensitivity—a. love b. receptivity c. interest d. talent
3. disillusioned—a. content b. rebellious c. talented d. disenchanted
4. conform—a. act the same b. act differently c. get rich d. study
5. destiny—a. past life b. fate c. mind d. ideas
6. abandon—a. take up b. study c. forget d. desert
7. obviously—a. generally b. clearly c. quickly d. later
8. renown—a. hate b. interest c. fame d. love
9. acclaim—a. interest b. dislike c. awards d. praise
10. lash out—a. attack b. praise c. study d. explain

B. Choose the phrase that best completes each sentence.

1. When he was a child, Limón considered ballet
   a. to be stupid
   b. to be for women only

c. to be uninteresting

d. all of the above

2. Limón grew up

a. dancing

b. in Mexico

c. in New York

d. loving music

3. Limón gave up art because

a. he preferred dancing

b. he was too poor to continue

c. he could not paint the way his teachers wanted

d. he didn't like painting

4. Limón was interested in

a. dancing

b. choreography

c. both a. and b.

d. neither a. nor b.

5. He thought Broadway musicals

a. didn't earn enough money for him

b. interfered with his serious work

c. were no fun

d. advertised rugs

6. Limón was recognized

a. as a great dancer

b. as a great painter

c. as a great musician

d. all of the above

C. Put these events in chronological order.

a. He gained national renown.

b. He changed his mind about dancing being an activity for men.

c. He made goodwill tours for the U.S. government.

d. His family moved to California.

e. He worked on Broadway shows.

f. He studied painting.

1.————2.————3.————4.————5.————6.————

D. Answer these questions.

1. Have you ever seen a ballet? Why do you think Limón considered ballet effeminate? Do you? Why?

2. Why did he leave art school? Do you think he should have tried to conform?

3. What were Limón's two goals?
4. Why did he stop doing Broadway musicals?
5. From what you read here, do you think Limón was a happy man when he died? Why or why not?

E. **From the list of words below choose the one that best fits in the blank in each sentence. Use each word only once.**

outstanding	devout
disillusioned	conform
destiny	abandon
commercial	acclaim

1. Limón quit art school because he did not want to _____ .
2. His mother was a _____ Catholic.
3. After quitting art school, he was _____ and unhappy.
4. Limón was an _____ dancer.
5. He won worldwide _____ for his dancing.
6. He worked on musicals in the 1930's but later decided to _____ this kind of work.
7. He saw a performance that changed his _____ .
8. He saw Broadway musicals as a _____ form of the art.

FÉLIX LOPE DE VEGA

A. **Choose the definition that means the same or most nearly the same as the first word.**
1. harmonious—a. orderly b. disorderly c. different d. odd
2. norm—a. act b. model c. figure d. difference
3. exert—a. remove b. put forth c. instruct d. watch
4. magnetic—a. true b. weak c. attractive d. horrible
5. ardent—a. cold b. meager c. long d. eager
6. mundane—a. secondary b. useless c. earthly d. priestly
7. fickle—a. steady b. childish c. annoying d. changeable
8. contrition—a. repentance b. complaining c. definition d. vulgarity
9. magnificent—a. confined b. distant c. lavish d. tangled
10. infatuated—a. foolish b. frustrated c. inflated d. in love

B. Complete each of the following sentences with the best answer.

1. Lope de Vega wrote many plays and poems,
   a. but he led a boring life
   b. but he never had any children
   c. and led a very exciting and passionate life
   d. and was excommunicated from the church
2. The phrase, "It's by Lope!" was the same as saying
   a. "It's terrible!"
   b. "It's foolish!"
   c. "It's mundane!"
   d. "It's magnificent!"
3. Lope's primary schooling took place at the cloisters of the Order of the Teatinos, which was a
   a. public school
   b. military school
   c. monastery
   d. theatrical school
4. At the age of twelve, Lope
   a. wrote his first novel
   b. ran away from the cloisters with a friend
   c. discovered a treasure
   d. joined a pirate ship
5. Lope's magnetic influence on women made them
   a. come to him
   b. fear him
   c. reject him
   d. all of the above
6. Lope bought a house in Madrid near Cervantes, who was his
   a. rival
   b. partner
   c. best friend
   d. uncle
7. Lope understood the sensitive and contradictory character of the Spanish people, particularly the
   a. aristocracy
   b. priests
   c. common folk
   d. wealthy merchants
8. Between loves and adventures, Lope never abandoned his greatest passion, which was his
   a. mother
   b. wife
   c. writing
   d. respect for religion

9. Lope's most representative works are the historical comedies based on
   a. his religious training
   b. actual events
   c. myths
   d. the Bible

C. Put the following events in chronological order.

a. Lope ran away from the cloisters.
b. He became a priest.
c. Lope underwent his primary schooling at the cloisters.
d. He became seriously ill and repented.
e. He enlisted in the Invincible Armada.
f. He died at his house in Madrid.

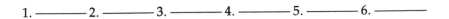

1. ——— 2. ——— 3. ——— 4. ——— 5. ——— 6. ———

D. Answer the following questions.

1. Who was Lope de Vega's biographer?
2. Who is considered the creator of the Spanish National Theatre?
3. Can you name five different types of writing for which Lope is famous?
4. What were his epic works based on?
5. Name three of Lope's historical comedies.
6. How was the new comedy different from comedy up until that point?
7. Why do you think Lope ran away from school at the cloisters? Have you ever wanted to run away from school? Tell why and describe your feelings.
8. The bishop of Avila encouraged Lope to study at the University of Alcalá. Has anyone influenced you to continue your education?
9. Describe Lope's personality. Why is he considered a man of contradictions?
10. Tell about a person you have known who is changeable and moody. Have you ever felt this way? Explain.

E. **Place the correct word from the list into the correct sentence.**

contemporaries   norms
diverse   privileges
magnetic   mundane
enhanced   refined
ardent   implacable

1. In *El arte nuevo de hacer comedias,* Lope de Vega introduced the use of different, or _____ metrical forms.
2. In his approach to women, Lope was bold and _____ .
3. His natural charm was intensified, or _____ by his lively eyes and smooth speech.
4. Lope drew women to him with his _____ personality.
5. Although he had joined the Church, Lope was unable to overcome his _____ desires for the things of this world.
6. Ordained a priest in 1616, Lope fell wildly in love with Marta Nevares de Santoyo, a sweet and _____ young comedienne.
7. Federico de Montalbán and Miguel de Cervantes were both _____ of Lope.
8. At his death, he was mourned not only by devoted friends, but also by people who had been his _____ enemies.
9. He defined the standards, or _____ for a new type of theatre.
10. He enjoyed many honors and _____ .

JOSÉ MARTÍ

A. **Choose the definition that means the same or most nearly the same as the first word.**

1. inspiring—a. dull b. cautious c. uplifting d. weighty
2. underground—a. secret b. dark c. mindless d. superior
3. sedition—a. ammunition b. insurrection c. allegiance d. hatred
4. quarry—a. institution b. mountain c. cave d. prey
5. firebrand—a. agitator b. lawyer c. cowboy d. businessman
6. fecundity—a. unproductive b. fatal c. clever d. productiveness
7. inquiry—a. answering b. questioning c. scheming d. poverty
8. rote—a. repetition b. surplus c. reason d. insight
9. outmoded—a. new b. practical c. topical d. unfashionable
10. confiscate—a. earn b. seize c. locate d. persevere

B. Complete each of the following sentences with the best answer.

1. According to the story, José Martí's main purpose in life was
   a. to write a great book or play
   b. to help Cuba gain independence
   c. to help reform prisons in Cuba
   d. to live a life of sacrifice

2. José Martí could be best described as
   a. a man of words, but no action
   b. a man of action, but no words
   c. a man of both words and action
   d. a man of lofty ideas, but little practical ability

3. While still a young lad in school, José was aware of Cuba's
   a. economy
   b. suffering
   c. relations with the U.S.
   d. Castro government

4. The young José was punished severely by the Spanish courts because
   a. they felt he was an idle, lazy boy
   b. he did not keep up with his studies
   c. he called for the overthrow of the Spanish government
   d. he disobeyed the school principal

5. After release from prison, Martí wanted to keep part of the chain with him because
   a. he was a pragmatist
   b. it helped him remember the suffering going on in Cuba
   c. it had sentimental value
   d. he thought it could help him escape

6. José was ordered to live in Spain so that
   a. he could not cause further trouble in Cuba
   b. he could go to a Spanish university
   c. he could feel sorry for his past conduct
   d. he could join the army

7. Throughout his busy life, the activity Martí loved best was
   a. organizing the Cuban Revolutionary Party
   b. writing poetry about Cuba
   c. writing for *The New York Sun* newspaper
   d. teaching young people

8. Márti died in battle because
   a. he wanted to be a hero
   b. the general ordered him to go beyond the front line
   c. he was old and suffered poor health
   d. he was willing to sacrifice his life for Cuban freedom

C. Put the following events in chronological order.

a. Martí came to New York.
b. Martí died in battle.
c. The Cuban Revolutionary Party was established.
d. The teenage José was deported to Spain.
e. Martí started an anti-Spanish newspaper when he was fifteen.

1. ————— 2. ————— 3. ————— 4. ————— 5. —————

D. Answer the following questions.

1. Why was Martí imprisoned when he was seventeen years old? Why did he want to keep a few chain links when he was finally released? Have you ever wanted to keep a particular object as a remembrance of a negative experience?

2. What did Martí mean when he said that book learning is not enough? "Young people have to learn to think for themselves and not believe without inquiry or speak without understanding what a man orders them to think and say." How do these ideas apply to you in today's world?

3. What kind of sacrifice did Martí have to make involving his wife and child? Have you ever had to sacrifice something that was very important to you in order to attain a particular goal? Explain your answer.

4. When Martí was attempting to bring about Cuban liberation, he stated, "Wait until the whole island is ready to rise as one man. To be able to wait is the greatest of virtues." Have you ever been in a situation or can you foresee a situation in which these words of caution might be valuable for your consideration? Explain.

5. In *La Guantanamera*, Martí wrote, *Y antes de morirme quiero/ Dejar mis versos del alma*. What do these words mean to you?

E. Select the word closest in meaning to the word in italics.

1. José Martí was a Cuban *patriot* who loved his country and longed for its freedom.
   a. patrician b. general c. nationalist d. father

2. At fifteen Martí was arrested for publishing a *clandestine* newspaper.
   a. destination b. unlawful c. humorous d. illiterate

3. Martí showed he was an *independent* thinker by speaking against the slavery of Spanish rule.
   a. free b. salaried c. profound d. unhappy

225

4. Martí was *exiled* from Cuba and forced to live in Spain.
   a. executed   b. banished   c. on vacation   d. traveling
5. Martí used his writing to *protest* the Spanish rule he hated so deeply.
   a. criticize   b. protect   c. accept   d. express
6. By being willing to die for the cause of Cuban freedom, Martí became a *martyr*.
   a. traitor   b. free man   c. saint   d. human sacrifice
7. While living in the United States, Martí worked hard to *rally* together all Cubans who were forced to leave Cuba.
   a. enjoy   b. socialize   c. unite   d. realize
8. Although he was not allowed to go home, Martí never forgot his *native* land, Cuba.
   a. birthplace   b. peasant   c. language   d. palm trees
9. Martí knew in advance that he would die when he spoke those *prophetic* words of his death.
   a. poetic   b. proper   c. fateful   d. professional
10. The battle of Dos Ríos *launched* Cuba's war for independence that lasted three more years.
    a. ended   b. started   c. interrupted   d. fed

GABRIELA MISTRAL

A. Choose the definition that means the same or most nearly the same as the first word.
1. keen—a. poor b. enthusiastic c. influential d. loving
2. serene—a. tall b. wealthy c. calm d. nervous
3. rustic—a. from the country b. urban c. stupid d. rich
4. perceptive—a. rich b. observant c. stupid d. tall
5. compel—a. discourage b. insist c. deny d. motivate
6. anguish—a. happiness b. content c. joy d. unhappiness
7. reared—a. raised b. seen c. hated d. killed
8. like wildfire—a. slowly b. happily c. fortunately d. very quickly
9. manifest—a. described b. shown c. written d. forgotten
10. remains—a. body b. books c. household possessions d. money

B. Complete each of the following sentences with the best answer.
1. The story implies that Gabriela Mistral was very
   a. perceptive
   b. insensitive

226

c. cruel

d. both b. and c.

2. The teacher who sent Gabriela home thought she was
   a. a poor student who should only be taught to cook and sew
   b. an outstanding student
   c. a natural poet
   d. an ill-mannered young woman

3. In the mining town where Gabriela first taught, the children
   a. were very rich
   b. were very unruly
   c. were very healthy
   d. had very little money to buy clothing

4. Gabriela's first book, *Desolación*, was inspired by
   a. Rubén Darío
   b. her lover, Romelio Ureta
   c. José Martí
   d. her father

5. The story implies that Rubén Darío felt that Gabriela was
   a. not a good poet
   b. an extremely gifted poet
   c. a poor student
   d. an egotist

6. El Instituto de las Españas of New York
   a. insulted her
   b. gave her a job
   c. refused to publish *Desolación*
   d. published *Desolación*

7. Gabriela was invited to Mexico to help
   a. cook and sew
   b. start a revolution
   c. teach adults
   d. organize public libraries

8. During the Spanish civil war, Gabriela went to
   a. Paris
   b. jail
   c. the mountains
   d. Cuba

9. In Paris, Gabriela was the guardian angel of
   a. other poets
   b. the French people
   c. the Spaniards in exile
   d. the French government

10. In 1945, Gabriela
    a. won the Nobel Prize for Literature
    b. won the Pulitzer Prize

c. married her lover

d. helped commemorate the Martí Centennial

C. Put the following events in chronological order.

a. Gabriela became principal of a school in a cold, deserted region of southern Chile.

b. She began to travel and lead a very active life.

c. The wasteland where she was living and her depression led her to write *Desolación*.

d. She was awarded the Nobel Prize for Literature in Sweden.

e. Gabriela was sent home for not being a good student.

f. Romelio Ureta committed suicide.

1. ———— 2. ———— 3. ———— 4. ———— 5. ———— 6. ————

D. Answer the following questions.

1. What was the name of Gabriela's first book of poetry?

2. Why was she inspired to write this first book of poetry?

3. What prize was she awarded in Santiago de Chile?

4. Who was the poet-hero of Cuba that she admired in her essay of 1953?

5. Why did Gabriela return to Chile in 1954?

6. When Gabriela was sent home from school, why did she refuse to do any housework? What does this reaction tell you about the kind of person she was?

7. What effect did Romelio Ureta have on Gabriela's life? Has anyone ever had such a great influence on you? Explain.

8. Why did Gabriela choose to work in a "cold, inhospitable region"?

9. Why do you think that Gabriela traveled to different countries? What is the value of traveling?

10. Why do you think that Gabriela wanted to be buried in Chile "facing the lofty pines"?

E. Add the correct prefix to the following words from the essay.

dis-   im-   in-   mis-   un-

Example: able *unable*

1. imposing
2. understand
3. guided
4. perceptive
5. prestigious
6. hospitable
7. decisive

Now give the dictionary meaning of each original word. How does the prefix change the meaning of each word?

RITA MORENO

A. **Choose the word that means the same or most nearly the same as the first word.**
1. gang—a. group b. girls c. troubles d. work
2. on all sides—a. in the streets b. at school c. everywhere d. at home
3. reveal—a. hide b. show c. develop d. stop
4. dubbed—a. showed b. bought c. re-recorded d. sold
5. landed (a role)—a. bought b. got c. wrote d. refused
6. guts—a. courage b. honesty c. beauty d. intelligence
7. anxious—a. reluctant b. happy c. sad d. eager
8. accolade—a. criticism b. praise c. review d. gift
9. made it—a. succeeded b. failed c. earned d. entered

B. **Choose the phrase that best completes each sentence.**
1. *West Side Story* was about
   a. the street life in New York
   b. Rita Moreno
   c. teenage gangs in New York
   d. the 1950's
2. Rita Moreno's native language is
   a. Spanish
   b. English
   c. French
   d. none of the above
3. She began performing
   a. when she was a teenager
   b. when her parents needed the money
   c. when she was a child
   d. at Bar Mitzvahs
4. She went to Hollywood because
   a. she was tired of New York
   b. she had a movie offer
   c. she couldn't get any work
   d. the story doesn't say
5. Moreno said that the role of Anita
   a. was easy
   b. was a very good one
   c. was a poor representation of a Latin woman
   d. was the only role of a Latin woman that she ever got
6. Rita Moreno has acted
   a. in films
   b. on Broadway

c. in London
d. all of the above
7. Rita Moreno feels that awards are important to her because
    a. they represent recognition of her talent
    b. they increase her opportunities
    c. they represent progress for all Latins
    d. all of the above

C. Put these events in chronological order.
a. She moved to New York.
b. She performed for the first time.
c. She won an Oscar.
d. She played in *The Ritz*.
e. She acted in London.
f. She appeared in *West Side Story*.

1.———2.———3.———4.———5.———6.———

D. Answer these questions.
1. Where was Rita Moreno born?
2. Where did she grow up?
3. What is her real name?
4. What are some jobs she has had?
5. Why was the part of Anita "fabulous"?
6. What award did she win for her performance in *The Ritz*?

E. Discuss these questions.
1. Rita Moreno changed her name. Many of the famous people you have read about have also changed their names. What are some possible reasons why people do this? Have you ever wanted to change your name? What would you change it to? Why did you choose that name?
2. Have you seen *West Side Story* or *The Ritz*? What did you think of the characters that Rita Moreno played? Can you remember some other films which had Latin characters? How were they portrayed?
3. Rita Moreno said, ". . . not many of us have really made it in both the Spanish-speaking and English-speaking worlds." Do you think this is true? Why or why not? How do you define "success" (making it)?

LUIS MUÑOZ MARÍN

A. Choose the definition that means the same or most nearly the same as the first word.
1. loyalty—a. annoyance b. faithfulness c. silliness d. awkwardness
2. discipline—a. control b. disorder c. paleness d. nerve
3. matriculate—a. leave b. enroll c. disregard d. come out
4. alliance—a. need b. association c. deed d. fort
5. corruption—a. morality b. standard c. opposition d. decay
6. irregularity—a. pattern b. inconsistency c. plan d. hope
7. redemption—a. deliverance b. call c. recall d. memory
8. furnish—a. provide b. equate c. join d. withdraw
9. erupt—a. take in b. drop c. stun d. explode
10. confer—a. imply b. explore c. consult d. insult

B. Complete each of the following sentences with the best answer.
1. Muñoz Marín's first job was as
    a. a journalist
    b. the secretary of the resident commissioner of Puerto Rico
    c. a poet
    d. Puerto Rico's first elected governor
2. Before he entered politics, Muñoz Marín believed that Puerto Rico should have
    a. independence
    b. commonwealth status
    c. statehood
    d. none of the above
3. Before Muñoz Marín became governor, Puerto Rico was governed by
    a. Spain
    b. the United States
    c. France
    d. Indians
4. Independence, as proposed by the Tydings Plan, would have been bad for Puerto Rico because
    a. it was too close to the United States
    b. its economy could not support the people
    c. the people did not want to be independent
    d. none of the above
5. Muñoz Marín worked hard to enable Puerto Rico to become
    a. illiterate
    b. rich
    c. a modern state
    d. a banana republic

6. The program for industrialization that Muñoz Marín started in 1944 was called
   a. Operation Popular Party
   b. Operation Puerto Rico
   c. Operation Bootstrap
   d. Operation Economy
7. When did Puerto Rico achieve commonwealth status?
   a. 1948
   b. 1944
   c. 1952
   d. never

C. **Put the following events in chronological order.**
   a. Muñoz Marín was elected senator.
   b. He attended school in Washington.
   c. He was introduced to American schools.
   d. He was elected Governor of Puerto Rico.
   e. He met Roosevelt.
   f. He resigned the governorship and was elected president of the Senate.

   1. ———— 2. ———— 3. ———— 4. ———— 5. ———— 6. ————

D. **Answer the following questions from the story as simply as possible.**
   1. When did Muñoz Marín first go to New York?
   2. Where did he receive most of his education?
   3. How did he support himself after his father died?
   4. How did he meet his wife?
   5. How did he get involved in Puerto Rican politics?
   6. What did he write about that so interested the American government?
   7. How did Muñoz Marín suggest that Puerto Rico could really best be helped?
   8. Why was Senator Tydings' plan so bad for Puerto Rico?
   9. Why was Muñoz Marín's plan called "Operation Bootstrap"?
   10. What did Congress finally do about the status of Puerto Rico?

E. **Use each of the following words in an original sentence. If you don't know the meaning, look it up in the dictionary.**
   1. moral
   2. principles
   3. virtues
   4. matriculate
   5. socialist

6. liberal
7. industrialization
8. protectorate
9. commonwealth
10. integrity

PABLO NERUDA

A. Choose the definition that means the same or most nearly the same as the first word.
1. lush—a. limited b. scarce c. meager d. rich
2. humid—a. old b. arid c. dry d. moist
3. enraged—a. amused b. angered c. satisfied d. pleased
4. toil—a. relaxation b. rest c. work d. playtime
5. dupe—a. cheat b. aid c. comfort d. entertain
6. ousted—a. forced out b. allowed out c. helped out d. followed out
7. coup—a. tragic event b. national cry c. government overthrow
          d. democratic election
8. reiterated—a. blocked b. repeated c. opened d. rejected
9. deliberate—a. careless b. careful c. quick d. spontaneous
10. jovial—a. depressed b. joyless c. joyful d. miserable

B. Complete each of the following sentences with the best answer.
1. The story is mainly about
   a. a poet
   b. a Chilean poet
   c. a communist
   d. a Nobel Prize-winning Chilean poet
2. Neruda often wrote about
   a. love
   b. his native land
   c. government
   d. all of the above
3. In 1936, Neruda joined other literary figures of the world in order to protest
   a. fascism
   b. democracy
   c. communism
   d. catholicism

4. The author implies that one of the reasons Neruda was not awarded the Nobel Prize twenty years earlier was because
   a. he did not deserve it
   b. he was not very popular
   c. his poetry was difficult to understand
   d. he was a communist
5. Salvador Allende's government had an unprecedented platform that called for
   a. a war with Spain
   b. the imprisonment of all communists
   c. a government in which all parties, except the communists, were represented
   d. a government in which all parties were represented
6. As a diplomat, Neruda
   a. represented his country abroad
   b. served in the Senate
   c. was a spokesman for the Communist Party
   d. served in the Russian Army
7. Neruda's personality can best be described as
   a. quiet and thoughtful
   b. inward and shy
   c. spiteful and sarcastic
   d. outgoing and magnetic

C. Put the following events in chronological order.
   a. Neruda was exiled from Chile.
   b. He became ill with cancer.
   c. He won the Nobel Prize.
   d. He became a communist.
   e. Allende's government was overthrown.
   f. The Spanish civil war began.

1. ——— 2. ——— 3. ——— 4. ——— 5. ——— 6. ———

D. Answer the following questions.
   1. In which countries did the young Neruda serve as a diplomat?
   2. What war marks the start of Neruda's active role in radical politics?
   3. Who was elected president of Chile in 1970?
   4. In what way was Allende's government unprecedented?
   5. What happened twelve days after Allende's government was overthrown?
   6. When Neruda was in his early twenties, he began his diplomatic career. If you could go on a diplomatic mission to another coun-

try, where would you go and what would you attempt to accomplish there?

7. Much of Neruda's poetry is satirical. What is the meaning of the term "satire"? Who were the objects of Neruda's satire? How do you think Neruda felt about the people whom he satirized? Do you think that he was trying to show them something about themselves? Explain.

8. In *Oda al gato,* why does Neruda call the cat *"conquistador sin patria, ... mínimo tigre de salón"?* What does the excerpt from this poem reveal about Neruda's feelings about animal life, or nature in general? Look back at the story to answer this question.

9. Why did Neruda anger so many people when he traveled to Russia? How did the Russians feel about him? How did the United States react to him? Do you think that the United States would react the same way today as they did then? Give reasons to support your answer.

10. What is the meaning of "vindicated"? Why did the intellectuals of the world feel vindicated when Neruda won the Nobel Prize in 1971? 1971?

E. **Write a composition of several paragraphs in which you include the following:**
   a. How did Neruda feel about his writing?
   b. Describe the activity in your life that you enjoy the most.
   c. How did you originally become involved in this activity?
   d. Tell how you feel when you are involved in this activity.
   e. Is there something about your personality that makes it seem natural for you to enjoy this activity so much, or are your feelings sometimes a surprise to you?
   f. Do you have any future plans that would involve this activity?

JOSÉ CLEMENTE OROZCO

A. **Choose the definition that means the same or most nearly the same as the first word.**
   1. devastating—a. harmless b. nearby c. destructive d. productive
   2. depict—a. challenge b. provoke c. portray d. distrust
   3. mural—a. wall painting b. fable c. story d. color
   4. awareness—a. ignorance b. stability c. stare d. alertness

5. fresco—a. painting on wood b. painting on plaster c. mobile
   d. brush
6. pigment—a. interpretation b. strangeness c. color d. laughter
7. scorn—a. stiffness b. contempt c. love d. apathy
8. intense—a. vague b. wet c. dry d. acute
9. mammoth—a. gigantic b. tiny c. secure d. bothersome

B. Complete each of the following sentences with the best answer.
1. Orozco wanted to paint murals because
   a. they were large
   b. they were easily seen
   c. they could be easily understood
   d. all of the above
2. Orozco decided to become a painter
   a. because it was fashionable
   b. to make money
   c. after he lost his left hand in an explosion
   d. because he wanted fame
3. In the early 1920s, Orozco was chosen by Mexico's government
   a. to decorate the walls of public buildings with frescoes
   b. to paint the members of the government
   c. to illustrate the Bible
   d. to decorate the *Rotunda de los Hombres Ilustres*
4. Most of Orozco's paintings depict
   a. the rich
   b. skyscrapers
   c. revolutionaries
   d. humble Indians and mestizos
5. Some upper-class Mexicans do not like Orozco's work because
   a. he criticized Mexican foreign policy
   b. he criticized the Church and the privileged classes
   c. he painted murals in the United States
   d. he criticized Father Hidalgo
6. Orozco could be characterized as
   a. vague
   b. talented but extremely sensitive
   c. friendly and open
   d. constantly happy
7. When Orozco died, the Congress
   a. ordered a statue erected in his honor
   b. confiscated his paintings
   c. declared two official days of mourning
   d. continued in session

C. Put the following events in chronological order.

a. Orozco's first major exhibit took place in Mexico City.
b. Orozco lost a hand.
c. He was picked to create a fresco at Mexico City's main high school.
d. He was criticized for being too hard on the Church and the wealthy.
e. He decided to become a painter.
f. He said it was unfair of critics to scorn and insult him.

1. ————— 2. ————— 3. ————— 4. ————— 5. ————— 6. —————

D. Answer the following questions as simply as possible.

1. How did Orozco describe his own paintings?
2. Why did he want to paint murals?
3. How did he lose his left hand?
4. On what kind of surface is a fresco painted?
5. What did most of Orozco's paintings depict?
6. What two things did Orozco hate?
7. Was Orozco an abstract or realistic painter?
8. Why do the common people love his murals?
9. When did he die?
10. What kind of buildings did he decorate?

E. Mark T in front of each statement that is true, and F in front of each statement that is false.

——— 1. Reformers and revolutionaries usually favor the policies of the government in power.
——— 2. Orozco said his paintings would replace the Bible.
——— 3. Orozco's first paintings showed strong social awareness.
——— 4. The government picked Orozco to do a fresco at the university in Mexico City.
——— 5. Orozco was a mestizo.
——— 6. Orozco was a realistic painter.
——— 7. Orozco's paintings pleased nearly all Mexicans.
——— 8. Orozco painted exclusively in Mexico.
——— 9. Orozco yearned to see an end to poverty and war.
——— 10. Orozco accepted criticism well.

OCTAVIO PAZ

A. Choose the definition that means the same or most nearly the same as the first word.
1. outskirts—a. closeness b. suburbs c. familiarity d. nearness
2. aloof—a. friendly b. confused c. distant d. angry
3. upheaval—a. distortion b. worship c. violent change d. sadness
4. atheist—a. unbeliever b. believer c. transmitter d. god
5. primary—a. indirect b. useful c. kind d. fundamental
6. excessive—a. modest b. extravagant c. harmful d. cheerful
7. passive—a. inactive b. concerned c. demanding d. active
8. indivisible—a. unsupported b. varied c. cheap d. inseparable
9. repression—a. strict restraint b. fairness c. leniency d. inactivity
10. simultaneous—a. at the same time b. happy c. harsh d. unlucky

B. Complete each of the following sentences with the best answer.
1. Paz's heritage is
   a. Spanish and French
   b. Spanish and Indian
   c. Spanish
   d. Indian
2. *Luna silvestre* was published when Paz was
   a. nineteen
   b. twenty-nine
   c. thirty-six
   d. forty
3. *Luna silvestre* is an ode to
   a. power
   b. imagination and love
   c. ideals
   d. both b. and c.
4. Paz went to Spain to fight the fascists in the Spanish civil war
   a. for money
   b. to escape the poverty of his own background
   c. because he was forced to
   d. to fulfill his vision of life
5. In *El laberinto de la soledad,* Paz concludes the Mexican has suffered too much from
   a. the Spanish conquest
   b. the grip of the clergy
   c. the exploitation by the rich
   d. all of the above
6. In his writings, Paz has *not* discussed
   a. world politics
   b. the architecture of Mexico

c. Eastern religions
d. the ancient myths of the Aztecs
7. Paz resigned as Mexico's ambassador to India
    a. to accept a position with Harvard University
    b. to protest the massacre of Tlatelolco
    c. to devote himself to writing
    d. to become ambassador to the United States

C. **Put the following events in chronological order.**
    a. Octavio Paz returned from Europe.
    b. He became a professor at Harvard.
    c. He married Marie Tramini.
    d. Five hundred Mexican students were shot down.
    f. Paz resigned his ambassadorship.

1. ——— 2. ——— 3. ——— 4. ——— 5. ———

D. **Answer the following questions as simply as possible.**
    1. How old was Octavio Paz when his first book was published?
    2. What was his father's profession?
    3. From what had Mexico suffered?
    4. How did Paz feel about his marriage?
    5. What does he prefer, writing or teaching?
    6. Whom did his father support in the revolution?
    7. Can you name three of Paz's books published since 1950?

E. **Answer the following questions.**
    1. To Octavio Paz, the most important things in life were love, ideas, and imagination. Describe one type of love (God, family, friends) and tell why it is important in your own life. How has this love affected you?
    2. Octavio Paz lived in India, where he studied Indian philosophy. He learned to "be silent and listen to his own heart." Try the following experiment and then be prepared to discuss your feelings and experiences. Sit completely alone in a dark and silent place. Do not move for at least ten minutes. Be aware of your body and thoughts, being calm at the same time. How did you feel and what did you think of? What pictures came into your mind? What did you feel like doing?
    3. What activity gives you the greatest happiness? Tell how you got interested in it and describe the activity in detail.
    4. Is having money important in your life? Explain.
    5. Do you think or feel there is a "God"? Why or why not?

PABLO PICASSO

A. Choose the definition that means the same or most nearly the same as the first word.
1. restless—a. at ease b. intelligent c. jittery d. famous
2. arrogant—a. humble b. crafty c. modest d. haughty
3. twist—a. turn b. robe c. plan d. tax
4. sphere—a. square b. globe c. geometry d. flavor
5. doormat—a. complainer b. uncomplaining sufferer c. romantic idealist d. friend
6. confidante—a. intimate friend b. betrayer c. lover d. interviewer
7. haven—a. city b. safe place c. heaven d. woods
8. contemplate—a. refuse b. sleep c. return d. consider
9. fury—a. rage b. glee c. peace d. prosperity

B. Complete each of the following sentences with the best answer.
1. Picasso produced
   a. paintings, sculptures, and poetry
   b. paintings, sculptures, and pottery
   c. paintings, book illustrations, and books
   d. sculptures, pottery, and books
2. Picasso first studied art
   a. with his father
   b. with a professor at Málaga University
   c. in art school
   d. by himself
3. Picasso
   a. dropped out of art school because of failure
   b. never went to school
   c. dropped out of school because he wanted to learn on his own
   d. did well in school
4. He used a blue color scheme throughout his early career because of
   a. artistic preference
   b. a lack of money
   c. French influence
   d. dreams about colors
5. He developed a new school of painting called
   a. modern art
   b. primitive art
   c. Cubism
   d. Spanish geometrical art

240

6. Picasso was
   a. anti-Nazi and pro-Communist
   b. pro-Nazi and anti-Communist
   c. pro-Communist and anti-American
   d. anti-Nazi and anti-Spanish
7. Guernica is the name of
   a. a town in Spain
   b. one of Picasso's lovers
   c. a famous painting by Picasso
   d. both a. and c.

C. Put the following events in the order in which they occurred.
   a. He went to art school.
   b. Picasso studied art with his father.
   c. Guernica was destroyed by the Nazi air force.
   d. He lived on the Left Bank in Paris.
   e. Picasso left Spain for good.

   1. ——— 2. ——— 3. ——— 4. ——— 5. ———

D. Answer the following questions as simply as possible.
   1. What was Picasso's lifestyle like?
   2. In which ways did he resemble other young Left Bank artists?
   3. How did he show his love for animals?
   4. In which ways was his last wife, Jacqueline, especially helpful in his career?
   5. What is Cubism?

E. Use each of the following words in a sentence. If you don't know the meanings, look them up in a dictionary.
   1. borrow
   2. fond
   3. cheapest
   4. however
   5. through
   6. fought
   7. high
   8. awoke

FELISA RINCÓN DE GAUTIER

A. Choose the definition that means the same or most nearly the same as the first word.

1. comply—a. disagree b. obey c. raise d. prepare
2. unwritten—a. loud b. peculiar c. implied d. secondary
3. slum—a. deterioration b. battle c. mansion d. honor
4. rickety—a. sound b. stable c. obvious d. shaky
5. malnutrition—a. science b. skeleton c. poor nourishment d. tower
6. underprivileged—a. deprived b. rejected c. fortunate d. noble
7. homesick—a. hidden b. calm c. longing for home d. disguised
8. permit—a. stock b. allow c. refuse d. cry
9. further—a. advance b. confer c. please d. agree with
10. constituents—a. areas b. voters c. fads d. rovers

B. Complete each of the following sentences with the best answer.

1. Felisa Rincón de Gautier took charge of her six brothers and sisters
   a. when she was thirteen years old
   b. when her mother died
   c. when her father died
   d. both a. and b.
2. When Felisa walked into La Perla, she entered
   a. a famous garden
   b. a restaurant
   c. a slum district
   d. a suburb of Mexico City
3. Felisa first campaigned politically
   a. for the United States Senate
   b. for governor of Puerto Rico
   c. to get women to vote
   d. for mayor of San Juan
4. Before really entering politics, Felisa went to New York and became a
   a. writer
   b. teacher
   c. dress designer
   d. beauty contest winner
5. Felisa met her husband-to-be
   a. in New York
   b. in La Perla
   c. while working in politics
   d. at her dress shop

6. Felisa decided to run for office because
   a. her husband died
   b. her husband and father allowed her to
   c. the people of Puerto Rico needed help
   d. she wanted the fame
7. She was mayor of San Juan for
   a. two years
   b. eight years
   c. twelve years
   d. twenty-two years

C. Put the following events in chronological order.

   a. Felisa Rincón voted for the first time.
   b. She went to New York to work.
   c. She met her future husband.
   d. She visited La Perla in San Juan.
   e. She formed a committee to help get women to vote.
   f. She was elected mayor of San Juan.

   1. ———— 2. ———— 3. ———— 4. ———— 5. ———— 6. ————

D. Answer the following questions from the story as simply as possible.

   1. When did the members of Felisa's family begin calling her "madrecita"?
   2. What did Felisa see in La Perla?
   3. What was the tragedy in Puerto Rico that inspired her to run for office?
   4. What did Felisa do every Wednesday at City Hall?
   5. Can you mention two things that she did to help the poor people of San Juan?
   6. "A woman should devote her life to her husband and children." Do you agree or disagree? Tell why.
   7. How many brothers or sisters do you have? How do you help them or look after them? Tell about your duties at home.
   8. Suppose that you lived in a slum, where the streets were made of mud, the houses were shacks, and your children were sick with malnutrition. What would you say to the mayor if you had a chance to tell her about your problems?
   9. Do you think that children should obey their parents at all times? Why or why not? Explain. Give examples.
   10. What woman do you admire greatly? Describe her.

LOLA RODRÍGUEZ DE TIÓ

A. Choose the definition that means the same or most nearly the same as the first word.

1. cultured—a. helpful b. refined c. awkward d. kind
2. atmosphere—a. surrounding influence b. attraction c. mildness d. disease
3. willpower—a. careful b. strength c. greedy d. strange
4. insist—a. retain b. keep c. lose d. state firmly
5. tresses—a. costumes b. makeup c. wishes d. hair
6. balustrade—a. river b. railing c. speech d. fire
7. splendor—a. dullness b. beauty c. worth d. value
8. individualistic—a. steady b. ill c. sweet d. unique
9. dissenter—a. group b. camp c. nonconformist d. agreement
10. tribute—a. praise b. criticism c. game d. plant

B. Complete each of the following sentences with the best answer.

1. As a girl, Lola Rodríguez de Tió left school and studied independently
   a. in rebellion against the school's strict discipline
   b. because she was not doing well enough to please her parents
   c. because education was limited for girls
   d. both a. and c.
2. When Lola first saw the man she eventually would marry,
   a. she hid from him in her room
   b. she loosened her hair
   c. she remarked to her sister that she would marry him
   d. she wrote him a love letter
3. Lola was the first Puerto Rican woman
   a. to leave school and study independently
   b. to wear short hair
   c. to publish a volume of poetry
   d. none of the above
4. She was the first author of the revolutionary song,
   a. *Mis cantares*
   b. *La borinqueña*
   c. *Claros y nieblas*
   d. *La Guantanamera*
5. Lola and her husband were exiled from Puerto Rico because
   a. they were married without permission
   b. they spoke up against slavery and in defense of free speech
   c. Lola received an award of merit from the government of Venezuela
   d. they joined Cuba's movement for independence

6. Lola Rodríguez de Tió worked not only for Puerto Rican independence, but also for
   a. Cuban independence
   b. Mexican independence
   c. Haitian independence
   d. Dominican independence
7. The Institute of Puerto Rican Culture
   a. published her complete works in five volumes
   b. awarded her numerous prizes
   c. exhibited her letters, manuscripts, pictures, and favorite objects
   d. all of the above

C. Put the following events in chronological order.
   a. She wrote the hymn, *La borinqueña*.
   b. She married Bonocio Tió Segarra.
   c. She honeymooned in Europe.
   d. She returned to Havana to live after her exile.
   e. She secured the release of Puerto Rican patriots.
   f. She published *Claros y nieblas*.

   1. ———— 2. ———— 3. ———— 4. ———— 5. ———— 6. ————

D. Answer the following questions as simply as possible.
   1. Where was Lola Rodríguez de Tió born?
   2. In what ways was she attractive?
   3. What was she against and what did she defend?
   4. Which two countries did she love very much?
   5. Where in South America did she and her husband live for a while?

E. Use each of the following words in a sentence. Look up the meanings that you don't know.
   1. impetuous
   2. tempered
   3. persecutions
   4. acclaim
   5. aspirations
   6. serene
   7. impulsive

DOMINGO SARMIENTO

A. Choose the definition that means the same or most nearly the same as the first word.

1. undertaking—a. support b. hill c. jump d. project
2. rigid—a. loose b. stiff c. false d. fine
3. progressive—a. advanced b. backward c. dark d. lazy
4. slope—a. slant b. line c. air d. top
5. constant—a. flexible b. steady c. childish d. horrible
6. tyranny—a. flavor b. food c. harshness d. fever
7. literacy—a. ability to read and write b. dryness c. shallowness d. exactness
8. sponsor—a. doctor b. teacher c. patron d. tyrant
9. keynote—a. middle b. bottom c. music d. central fact
10. strenuous—a. easy b. able c. poor d. arduous

B. Complete each of the following sentences with the best answer.

1. Domingo Sarmiento believed that underprivileged people should have
   a. fewer rights than others
   b. the same rights as others
   c. more rights than others
   d. no rights at all
2. Before Sarmiento was able to make changes, women in Latin America generally did not
   a. go to school
   b. get married
   c. have the same rights as men
   d. both a. and c.
3. Sarmiento wanted an enlightened society in which
   a. people would learn how to help themselves
   b. everyone would be educated
   c. no one would have to work
   d. both a. and b.
4. Democracy is government
   a. by the people
   b. by the military
   c. by the president
   d. by a few people
5. In order to spread his ideas, Sarmiento started a
   a. newspaper
   b. school
   c. factory
   d. railroad company

6. Sarmiento's parents believed that the only path to democracy was
   a. friendship
   b. a large family
   c. education
   d. the use of force
7. During the emerging dictatorship of Juan Manuel Rosas, Sarmiento expressed his personal views and was almost
   a. imprisoned
   b. executed
   c. befriended by the dictator
   d. made Rosas' assistant
8. Sarmiento used a large part of his salary to
   a. bribe Rosas
   b. travel
   c. learn English
   d. develop his political career
9. When Sarmiento was elected president of Argentina *in absentia,*
   a. he was not in Argentina at the time
   b. he was living in Argentina
   c. he refused to accept the position
   d. he pardoned everyone in prison
10. While Sarmiento was president of Argentina, he
   a. ended the war with Paraguay
   b. started military and naval schools
   c. sponsored many public works
   d. all of the above

C. Put the following events in chronological order.
   a. Sarmiento was elected president of Argentina *in absentia.*
   b. He started Argentina's first school for girls.
   c. Sarmiento escaped from Argentina with his family and went to Chile.
   d. He was almost executed by Juan Manuel Rosas.
   e. Sarmiento was elected as "first citizen" of his school government.
   f. Facundo Quiroga, the Argentine dictator, was assassinated.

1. ——— 2. ——— 3. ——— 4. ——— 5. ——— 6. ———

D. Answer the following questions.
   1. Who was the Great Latin American Educator?
   2. What five general groups of underprivileged people did Sarmiento help?
   3. What happened in school that marked the beginning of his political career?

4. Whose biography inspired him to become a leader?
5. What similarities did Sarmiento find between himself and Benjamin Franklin?
6. What does this statement mean to you? "Ideas, sir, have no country."
7. Why was Sarmiento fired from his teaching job by the governor? Have you ever risked anything for your beliefs? Explain.
8. How do you think Sarmiento felt when he was elected president of Argentina *in absentia?*
9. How did Sarmiento feel about being a student in a classroom?
10. How do you feel about your own experience as a student? Have you ever felt differently? Explain.

E. **Indicate whether the following statements are** *fact* **or** *opinion*.
1. Sarmiento was the greatest Latin American educator of all time.
2. At a certain time in his life, Sarmiento got up every morning at 2:00 A.M. to study English.
3. Sarmiento's father was one of San Martín's soldiers.
4. In 1835, Facundo Quiroga was assassinated.
5. Horace Mann was the most important educator in the history of the United States.

PANCHO VILLA

A. **Choose the word that means the same or most nearly the same as the first word.**
1. controversy—a. agreement b. disagreement c. popular d. famous
2. idol—a. god b. enemy c. helper d. spokesman
3. bandit—a. hero b. idealist c. revolutionary d. robber
4. culprit—a. god b. victim c. innocent one d. guilty one
5. cattle rustler—a. one who takes care of cattle b. one who steals cattle c. one who kills cattle d. one who buys cattle
6. tactics—a. style b. strategies c. medals d. songs
7. at odds with—a. disagreeing with b. agreeing with c. disliked d. admired
8. conventional—a. cowardly b. daring c. revolutionary d. customary
9. ambush—a. meeting b. town c. surprise attack d. battle
10. six-shooter—a. knife b. gun c. beer d. package of cigarettes

B. Choose the phrase that best completes each sentence.

1. In the United States people think of Pancho Villa
   a. with love
   b. as a hero
   c. as a robber
   d. with great fear
2. When he was young, Villa
   a. never got into trouble
   b. was very religious
   c. was very rich
   d. was often in trouble
3. After escaping from jail the first time, Villa
   a. became a robber
   b. became a Mexican soldier
   c. was shot
   d. became a revolutionary
4. He learned military strategy
   a. in the Mexican army
   b. in the American army
   c. as a cattle rustler
   d. from studying books in jail
5. Villa was popular with the poor because
   a. he robbed them
   b. he sometimes gave them money stolen from the rich
   c. he was handsome
   d. he was pursued by the American army
6. The American army tried to capture Villa because
   a. he was a cattle rustler
   b. he was a revolutionary
   c. they wanted to aid the Mexican government
   d. he had attacked an American town
7. During this revolution in Mexico there was conflict between
   a. the Spanish and the Mexicans
   b. Americans and revolutionaries
   c. the government and the Mexican people
   d. all of the above
8. Villa retired because
   a. the revolution was won
   b. the revolution was lost
   c. he was tired of fighting
   d. the president gave him money to stop fighting
9. Villa was killed
   a. at home
   b. in an ambush

    c. by Americans

    d. by order of the Mexican government

C. Put these events in chronological order.

    a. Villa killed the man who raped his sister.

    b. He retired.

    c. He was in the American army.

    d. He was chased by the American army.

    e. He became a cattle rustler.

    f. He began to fight for the revolution.

1.————2.————3.————4.————5.————6.————

D. Answer these questions.

    1. How did Pancho Villa get his name?

    2. What kind of childhood did he have?

    3. Where was he in 1910?

    4. During his second stay in jail, how did he spend his time?

    5. How did his troops feel about him?

    6. How did other revolutionaries feel about him?

    7. Why did the American army stop trying to capture Villa?

    8. How did Villa live after his retirement?

E. Discuss these questions.

    1. Reread the quotation of the American reporter. Is this a flattering description? Would you like to have met Pancho Villa?

    2. What do you think Villa's ideals were? What were some of the ideals of other revolutionaries you have read about? What are your ideals?

    3. Why did the poor people of Mexico idolize Pancho Villa? Why did the middle-class revolutionaries dislike him? How do you feel about him?

EMILIANO ZAPATA

A. Choose the definition that means the *opposite* or most nearly *opposite* of the first word.

    1. freedom—a. liberty b. license c. subordination d. independence

    2. corrupt—a. wicked b. impure c. innocent d. rotten

    3. humble—a. vain b. unassuming c. meek d. poor

    4. privileged—a. restrained b. favored c. immune d. exceptional

    5. skilled—a. ready b. clever c. untrained d. able

6. fiery—a. even-tempered b. blazing c. hot-tempered d. inflamed
7. vanity—a. immodesty b. self-praise c. pride d. modesty
8. rumor—a. report b. gossip c. hearsay d. fact
9. ceremonial—a. casual b. unusual c. formal d. ritualistic
10. glory—a. obscurity b. fame c. honor d. dignity

B. Complete each of the following sentences with the best answer.
1. The best title for this story is
   a. "The Mexican Revolution"
   b. "The Zapatistas"
   c. "The Killing of Zapata"
   d. "Zapata: Dedicated Revolutionary"
2. Zapata was different from most other leaders because
   a. he was poor
   b. he was part Indian
   c. he refused to accept payoffs
   d. his father owned a small farm
3. A rich landowner sent Zapata to Mexico City
   a. for a vacation
   b. to deliver a message
   c. because he knew a lot about horses
   d. because he was a troublemaker and the landowner feared him
4. It doesn't say so in the story, but Zapata probably did not want to
   a. kill anyone
   b. continue his education
   c. be president
   d. eat Mexican food
5. One of Zapata's sayings, "Men of the South, it is better to die on your feet than to live on your knees," means
   a. it is better to wear out the soles on your shoes than injure your knees
   b. dying a free man is better than living like a slave
   c. compromise is better than death
   d. bravery means nothing if you lose your life
6. Zapata was killed by
   a. his own men
   b. accident
   c. food poisoning
   d. trickery
7. Some Mexican villagers believe that
   a. Zapata abandoned his cause to live in peace in the mountains
   b. Zapata was killed by his own men
   c. Zapata is still alive
   d. Zapata killed himself

C. Put the following events in chronological order.

a. Emiliano was elected the village leader.
b. The plan of Ayala was worked out.
c. Zapata's father died.
d. Zapata was murdered by a government colonel.
e. Zapata was sent to Mexico City by a rich landowner.
f. Zapata refused to pose in the president's chair.

1. ——— 2. ——— 3. ——— 4. ——— 5. ——— 6. ———

D. Answer the following questions from the story as simply as possible.

1. In what year did Mexico's Revolution begin?
2. What did the greedy government officials demand before giving fair treatment?
3. Where was Zapata born?
4. What is a mestizo?
5. What had been stolen from Emiliano and his brother?
6. Why did Zapata begin to gather an armed band of men?
7. What were Emiliano's fighters officially known as?
8. What didn't he want his men to become?
9. Why was Zapata lured into Colonel Guajardo's trap?
10. What color scarf did he wear?

PICTURE CREDITS